THE ELEMENT GUIDE

ANXIETY, PHOBIAS & PANIC ATTACKS

Elaine Sheehan is qualified in Applied Psychology and clinically trained in both hypnotherapy and psychotherapy. In addition to running a busy private practice, she frequently works for major corporate bodies and community and mental health services. She is currently designing her own courses for use in these fields. She has worked as a lecturer and trainer of therapists with British Hypnosis Research, running courses and workshops in hospitals across the UK. She is also the author of *Health Essentials: Self-Hypnosis* (Element).

Elaine Sheehan is registered with and can be contacted through The Hypnotherapy Register held by the National Council of Psychotherapists, 46 Oxhey Road, Watford, Herts, WD1 4QQ, UK. Tel. 01923 227772.

• THE ELEMENT GUIDE •

ANXIETY, PHOBIAS & PANIC ATTACKS

Your Questions Answered

Elaine Sheehan

E L E M E N T

Shaftesbury, Dorset ● Rockport, Massachusetts
Brisbane, Queensland

Text © Elaine Sheehan 1996

First published in Great Britain in 1996 by
Element Books Limited
Shaftesbury, Dorset SP7 8BP

Published in the USA in 1996 by
Element Books, Inc.
PO Box 830, Rockport, MA 01966

Published in Australia in 1996 by
Element Books Limited
for Jacaranda Wiley Limited
33 Park Road, Milton, Brisbane 4064

Cover design by Max Fairbrother
Text design by Roger Lightfoot
Typeset by Footnote Graphics, Warminster, Wiltshire
Printed and bound in Great Britain by Biddles Ltd,
Guildford and King's Lynn

British Library Cataloguing in Publication
data available

Library of Congress Cataloging in Publication
data available

ISBN 1–85230–773–0

Note from the Publisher
Any information given in any book in *The Element Guide* series is not
intended to be taken as a replacement for medical advice. Any person
with a condition requiring medical attention should consult a qualified
medical practitioner or suitable therapist.

Dedicated to my husband Mark

Acknowledgements

I am grateful to my teachers and particularly my clients, recovered and recovering, who are an invaluable source of further learning. Special thanks are due to those who allowed me to quote them in this work. (False names have been used to protect their identities.) I would also like to acknowledge my debt to my husband, Dr Mark Sheehan, for his support during the writing of this book, and for his contribution of the section on acupressure (Chapter 9).

Contents

Introduction   ix
1   The Nature of Anxiety   1
2   What are the Causes of Anxiety Disorders?   9
3   Paving the Way for Success   19
4   Taking Responsibility for Yourself and Your
    Thoughts   27
5   Using your Imagination   39
6   Relaxation and Self-hypnosis   49
7   Confronting Anxiety   61
8   Exploring Deeper   75
9   Further Ways to Help You Capture a Sense of
    Freedom   83
10 Help from Professionals and Friends   93
    Further Reading   101
    Useful Addresses   105
    Index   109

I really do believe these techniques have totally changed my life. I am feeling much happier and confident about the future.

Julia

Introduction

The spirit of self-help is the root of all genuine growth in the individual ... help from within invariably invigorates.

Samuel Smiles

The manifestations of anxiety may range from mild apprehension to fully-fledged panic attacks and phobias. Because it influences all of our lives to a certain extent, anyone can benefit from this book. Self-management is worth considering when your problem is not too severe or professional therapists are not readily available, or if you are just interested to see how much you can improve things by yourself.

The aim of this book is not to abolish anxiety completely. That should not, and indeed cannot, be done. A certain amount of anxiety in life is helpful, spurring us on to deal with the problems underlying our tensions. The main objective of this piece of work is to help you develop your own coping mechanisms for life, so that anxiety can be kept under control, at a reasonable, healthy level.

CHAPTER 1

The Nature of Anxiety

The mass of mankind live lives of quiet desperation.
                                        Henry David Thoreau

Anxiety has often been described as a modern phe-
nomenon. It is certainly true that we are now more than
ever aware of the effects it can have on our lives. From
time to time we all feel anxious; no one is immune. The
level of anxiety an individual is experiencing at any one
time will be reflected in that person's behaviour. Depending on the degree of anxiety, the effect may be positive or
negative.

As shown in figure 1, mild degrees of anxiety can serve
to enhance our behaviour, or more specifically in the case
of a particular task, our performance. Performance
improves proportionately with an increase in anxiety until
a certain level is reached, after which further anxiety
causes a complete disintegration in performance. Severe
degrees of anxiety can therefore be seen to have a
markedly disabling effect on behaviour.

THE 'FIGHT-OR-FLIGHT' RESPONSE AND ANXIETY

When faced with adversity the normal universal response
of the body is to prepare itself for action: to either confront

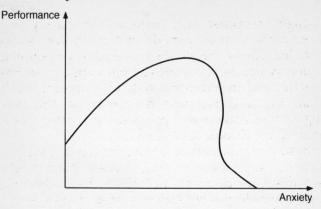

Figure 1   The relationship between anxiety and performance
(Yerkes-Dodson law, 1908)

or escape from danger. This is termed the 'fight-or-flight' response. It is an essentially protective reaction stimulating the sympathetic nervous system (part of the autonomic nervous system), triggering physical responses such as a change in the breathing pattern, an increase in heart rate and tension of the muscles. This can come about in anticipation of any perceived threat whether it be physical, psychological or imaginary.

When faced with *real* imminent danger, requiring quick and effective action (for example, being attacked by someone on the street), the 'fight-or flight' response is an appropriate and helpful one. However, there are times when it can be triggered in the body inappropriately. In the world we live in there are a range of potential threats which are long-term in nature (for instance, the stress caused by lack of job security, and financial pressures). Immediate action and a quick resolution of the situation is usually not an option in such circumstances, and therefore persistent attempts to cope by way of the 'fight-or-flight' response are not only unwarranted but can result in unnecessary strain being placed on the body.

For some people this inappropriate triggering of the

'fight-or-flight' response only happens periodically, and merely amounts to brief periods of tension and strain. However, for others this is their everyday response to stress. Their sympathetic nervous systems appear particularly sensitive and in a constant state of readiness, resulting in an identical response to events or situations requiring instant action, and persistent perceived stress. This can lead to a chronic state of anxiety.

The physical manifestations of anxiety can include palpitations, chest tightness, sweating, dryness of the mouth, increased desire to defaecate or urinate, headaches and dizziness. Psychologically, sufferers often report symptoms such as feelings of fear, panic and apprehension coupled with the tendency for themes of misfortune to dominate their thoughts (cognitions).

ANXIETY DISORDERS

When a person develops recurrent physical and psychological manifestations of anxiety in the absence of a proportionate provocative stimulus, they are likely to have an anxiety disorder. Stafford-Clark *et al* (1990) define an anxiety disorder as follows: 'A state of continual irrational anxiety and apprehension, sometimes flaring up into acute fear amounting to panic, accompanied by symptoms of autonomic disturbance; with secondary effects on such other mental functions as concentration, attention, memory and judgement.'

The authors of the *Diagnostic and Statistical Manual of Mental Disorders III* (1987) estimated that 2 to 4 per cent of the general population at one time or another experienced an anxiety disorder. We will now explore five such disorders in some detail: generalized anxiety disorder, panic disorder, panic disorder with agoraphobia, social phobia and simple phobia.

Generalized Anxiety Disorder (GAD)

I used to describe myself as a 'born worrier'. I was forever thinking 'what if', and waiting for things to go wrong. In reality, events would never prove quite as bad as I had feared. However, this did not stop me avoiding whenever possible situations that could potentially prove stressful.

John

GAD involves the experience of persistently high levels of anxiety over a period longer than six months in duration. Symptoms can include chronic muscular tension, self-perpetuating hyperactivity, repeated unrealistic worrying thoughts and apprehensive expectation. Generally the anxious focus is on two or more life circumstances such as work, finances or illness. Even though anxiety levels will fluctuate, some days being better than others, it is always in the back of the person's mind. Individuals with GAD often suffer from low self-esteem, and they can be particularly sensitive to being criticized, rejected or ignored.

GAD sufferers generally demonstrate poor coping behaviour in life. They tend to practise excessive avoidance of situations which may cause anxiety. It may also be that the focusing upon unrealistic worrying thoughts is a means of avoidance, distracting from images and thoughts of a feared situation or realistic problem. This would then prevent effective emotional processing, which in turn would help to maintain the generalized anxiety.

Panic Disorder

Every night I would sleep with the television and bedroom light on. This was in an attempt to take my mind off the panic attacks that would take over my entire being. My heart would race so fast and hard that it felt as though it was going to jump out of my body. I would be breathless and get hot and cold sweats. I felt I was so alone and that no one else could possibly be going through what I was. It is almost impossible for someone to begin to understand what it feels like if they have not experienced it themselves.

Catherine

A panic attack involves the inappropriate experience of a heightened state of arousal which the body would normally produce in preparation for confronting or fleeing real danger. This over-reactive response of the autonomic nervous system can cause the sufferer to experience the physical symptoms associated with 'fight-or-flight' in quite harmless everyday situations.

Panic attacks can occur in response to particular objects, activities or situations in phobic disorders. However, they can also arise without any external stimulus in sufferers of phobic disorders and those with panic disorder. This is why many people believe that panic attacks may be biological in origin.

Coryell and Winkur (1991) note that there is strong evidence to suggest that many, perhaps even most, panic attacks are caused by internal psychological patterns of thought. For instance, many sufferers become very tense by thinking about fear-provoking situations in advance, and by nervously anticipating the next panic attack ('fear of fear'). They can also be inclined to interpret the processes happening within their bodies in an irrational and catastrophic manner. This can result in problems such as a fear of fainting, or a fear of losing control and embarrassing themselves, or even a fear of having a heart attack and dying.

As the person with panic disorder becomes more and more preoccupied with bodily sensations, a vicious circle of anxiety can be created. For example, as seen in figure 2, if palpitations are experienced the sufferer may interpret this as a sign that a heart attack is imminent. This serves to create more anxiety, which in turn can lead to an increase in palpitations.

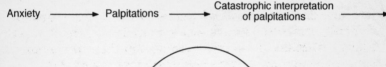

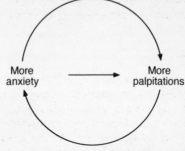

Figure 2 The vicious circle of anxiety caused by misinterpretation of bodily sensations such as palpitations

Panic Disorder with Agoraphobia

Within a couple of months of experiencing my first panic attack I was unable to lead a 'normal' life. In everyday situations such as in the supermarket or a restaurant my mind would fill with apprehensive thoughts, my heart would beat fast and I would feel the need to leave wherever I was and go to the toilet. Eventually, I began to avoid going out altogether. I could not face work or even the company of friends. Everything seemed too much. I felt I was going insane. The worst thing was not knowing, not understanding what was happening to me.

David

Phobias can be defined as excessive, unrealistic, uncontrollable fears which are triggered off by particular objects, activities or situations. They differ from ordinary fear in that they persist over a long period of time, are irrational and involve avoidance of the triggers. The term 'agoraphobia' originates from the Greek words *phobos* ('panic fear') and *agora* ('market place'), and thus can be translated as a 'fear of public places'. It is also common for sufferers to experience panic attacks.

In comparison with other phobic states agoraphobia involves a more general sense of insecurity. There is a fear and avoidance of crowded places where escape may be difficult, or isolated places where there is no help at hand. Many sufferers can become prisoners in their own homes; some even become afraid of being on their own there.

Social phobia

I had a blushing problem and used to feel self-conscious in all social situations. I presumed everyone was looking at me, thinking I was silly and stupid. I would carefully analyse in my head beforehand any contributions I would make to the conversation. Most of the time, however, I would just sit there feeling I had nothing to say and working out how I could make an escape without drawing too much attention to myself. It even came to a stage where I avoided going to the supermarket in case I bumped into someone I knew.

Jean

People with social phobia experience a fear of various situations which involve other people. The most common feature of this phobia is the fear of embarrassing oneself or becoming visibly anxious while under the observation of other people. Some sufferers can also experience panic attacks. Activities such as attending restaurants, bars or parties may be avoided.

Simple Phobia

I have been nervous of flying for as long as I could remember. I think one of the reasons for this was that my father was afraid of flying. The first time I ever went on a plane I was 21 years old. It was a flight to Portugal and I dealt with it by having several alcoholic drinks! I managed to avoid a holiday the following year because I had a baby and we couldn't really afford it. The year after that we went to Portugal again. This time I found the experience even worse because I knew in advance how awful the flight was going to be. After that things became so bad that I began to avoid flying completely. Each year we would go on a camping holiday in France. I was quite happy to travel by ferry, but dreaded ever having to fly again.

Angela

Simple phobia involves fear being directed towards one specific object, activity or situation, which is then avoided. Such a phobia tends not to interfere with a person's life to any great extent. For some reason simple phobias always seem to be given complicated sounding names! Some of the most common are listed in figure 3.

Phobia name	Fear
Acrophobia	Heights
Aerophobia	Flying
Ailurophobia	Cats
Arachnophobia	Spiders
Astrophobia	Lightning
Belonophobia	Needles
Claustrophobia	Enclosed spaces
Hematophobia	Blood
Hippophobia	Horses
Musophobia	Mice
Scholionophobia	School

Figure 3 Some common simple phobias

CHAPTER 2

What are the Causes of Anxiety Disorders?

Unhappiness, anxiety and depression are now more common than at any previous time in our history.

Vernon Coleman

There is no single satisfactory explanation for the occurrence of anxiety disorders. In attempting to understand how they develop a number of factors need to be explored. These include genetic predisposition, early upbringing, inner conflicts, anxiety as a learned response, physical factors, self-talk, coping behaviour and social determinants. The best explanation for the causes of anxiety disorders will more than likely take all these factors into account.

Genetic predisposition

Reviewing the relevant literature, Snaith (1991) concludes that research is suggesting that there may well be an inherited component of susceptibility to anxiety. The more 'vulnerable' an individual is in this respect, the less stress will be required to precipitate an anxiety disorder. For some people everyday stress may be enough to trigger severe anxiety. For those who do not have such a predisposition, extreme stress will be necessary before an anxiety state will develop.

Early upbringing

The capacity to combat stress can also be influenced by your upbringing. For example, if parents are insecure and overprotective, and consider the world a frightening place to live in, this may result in their children experiencing irrational fears. Failure to form an affectionate attachment to one or more primary persons in early years can result in perpetual anxiety regarding abandonment or rejection (Bowlby, 1973).

Inner conflicts

Psychoanalytic theory, which originates in the work of Freud, suggests that anxiety arises when there is inner conflict between instinct and social training and conscience. This conflict may or may not be consciously known to the sufferer. Phobias may be a symbolic representation of the resulting inner turmoil. Poor coping skills can lead individuals to a position where they attempt to ignore or deny the conflict. The anxiety associated with the conflict is then linked to an external object, activity or situation which is more easily avoidable.

Anxiety as a learnt response

In the case of phobic anxiety disorders in particular, it may be that for some people an unpleasant, frightening or traumatic event is associated with the onset of the phobia. In this way a fearful response can, by conditioning, become attached to a stimulus which we would not normally expect to provoke an anxiety response.

Psychologists refer to the process that takes place when an organism learns that two stimuli tend to go together as 'classical conditioning'. At the beginning of this century some very interesting experiments were conducted in this area by the Russian Nobel Prize winner Ivan Pavlov. He noted how a dog could learn to associate the sight of a food dish with the taste of food. On seeing the dish the dog would salivate, a response usually made when food is placed in its mouth. Pavlov then tested and demonstrated that a dog could be taught to associate food with other stimuli.

One of Pavlov's experiments involved turning on a light, to which the dog made no salivation response. After a very short time meat powder was presented to and then eaten by the dog. Salivation was recorded. Having repeated this process many times, the light was then turned on but no food was delivered. The dog salivated regardless. The light, which ordinarily would not produce a salivation response, had become associated with the meat powder.

A study (the ethics of which are questionable) which specifically demonstrates how a phobia can develop through classical conditioning was carried out by Watson and Raynor (1920). Albert, an eleven-month-old infant, showed great pleasure when presented with a white rabbit. As he played happily with the animal the experimenters repeatedly made a very loud noise behind Albert's head. Each time this noise frightened him and made him cry. The rabbit was eventually taken away. A little later when he was brought back to be played with again, Albert's response was to cry. The rabbit, which had produced a reaction of pleasure initially, had now become associated with the fear of the loud noise.

Although some phobias may well develop through conditioning, this theory of simple pairing of situation and traumatic event does not seem to offer a satisfactory explanation for all phobias.

Physical factors

Any physical illness may generate a feeling of anxiety. This is a natural reaction. Once the condition is diagnosed and treated appropriately, then anxiety about it can decrease. However, certain illnesses/drugs may in themselves increase the effects of the sympathetic nervous system, and therefore give the physical manifestations of anxiety. For instance:

- The heart condition of cardiac failure may cause palpitations and shortness of breath. Also benign paroxysmal tachycardia involves the heart rate periodically speeding up.
- Certain metabolic states (such as low blood sugar, metabolic acidosis) can cause severe inappropriate over-secretion of sweat (hyperhidrosis).
- Endocrine imbalances (such as an over-active thyroid gland) can cause palpitations.
- Certain drugs can cause symptoms similar to those experienced by anxiety disorder sufferers: for example, centrally acting appetite suppressants (for instance, diethylpropion and phentermine), and other central nervous system stimulants (such as caffeine).

Self-talk

A person's self-talk, and the way in which he or she structures their world, can greatly influence mood and behaviour. In general, those with an anxiety disorder tend to talk to themselves in a negative and anxious manner. For instance, in the section on 'generalized anxiety' it was noted how the persistent focus on repeated unrealistic worrying thoughts can, at the very least, help to maintain the disorder. Also, as was discussed in the section on 'panic disorder', certain individuals seem inclined to focus more on personal thoughts and body processes than on the external world. Frightening thoughts of what might happen, rather than actual events, trigger the anxiety and panic.

Whether or not there is a physical component to an initial panic attack, it would certainly appear that apprehensive anticipation of the next attack, and irrational and fearful thoughts about bodily sensations, can create a vicious circle of anxiety, and therefore promote further panic attacks. This is supported by a study conducted at the time of writing by Clark *et al* (1994). This work concluded that the misinterpretation of bodily sensations is the most significant predictor of subsequent symptoms and relapse in patients with this form of anxiety disorder.

Coping behaviour

Those suffering with anxiety disorders generally demonstrate poor coping behaviour. Rather than confronting the issues of their distress, avoidance is practised. Such behaviour only provides temporary relief, and in the long run serves to make things more difficult. Anxiety or panic-avoidance cycles may develop. Avoidance can breed more fear and anxiety, which in turn promotes further avoidance. If those close to the individual tolerate their restricted lifestyle, avoidance behaviour may become an easy option.

Social determinants

However robust an individual may appear, if sufficient stress is loaded on to them over time a point may be reached where they feel unable to cope any longer. Stress is particularly evident in times of change where the invariable accompanying upheaval to our world has to be dealt with. It is interesting in this respect to look at the life event rating scale constructed in 1967 by Holmes and Rahe (*see*

Life event	Score
Death of spouse	100
Divorce	73
Marital separation	65
Prison or mental hospital confinement	63
Death of a close family member	63
Major injury/illness	53
Marriage	50
Being fired	47
Marital reconciliation	45
Retirement	45
Major change in health or behaviour of a family member	44
Pregnancy	40
Sexual difficulties	39
Adding to family (eg through birth, adoption, relation moving in)	39
Major business readjustments	39
Major change in financial state	38
Death of a close friend	36
Changing line of work	36
Major change in number of arguments with spouse	35
Taking on mortgage, purchasing home, business etc	31
Foreclosure on a mortgage or loan	30
Major change in job responsibility	29
Son/daughter leaving home	29
In-law trouble	29
Outstanding personal achievement	28
Wife beginning/ceasing work outside home	26
Beginning/ceasing formal schooling	26
Major change in living conditions	25
Revision of personal habits	24
Troubles with the boss	23
Major change in working hours/conditions	20
Change in residence	20
Changing to a new school	20
Major change in recreation	19
Major change in church activities	19
Major change in social activities	18
Taking on loan less than £5,000	17
Major change in sleeping habits	16
Major change in number of family get-togethers	15
Major change in eating habits	15
Holidays	13
Christmas	12
Minor violations of the law	11

Figure 4 Life Event Scale (Reprinted with permission from the Journal of Psychosomatic Research, Vol II, Holmes and Rahe, 'The Social Readjustment Rating Scale', 1967, Elsevier Science Ltd, Pergamon Imprint, Oxford, England.)

figure 4) which scores various life events in accordance with the degree they can disrupt a person's life.

The relative importance of life events in the causation of anxiety disorders is controversial. It probably depends on an individual's vulnerability to stress, which in turn will be influenced by life circumstances and the other factors we have already discussed. More than likely certain life events may act as the 'straw that breaks the camel's back'.

Many patients come to my office asking the question: 'Why am I this way?' It is not always possible to trace anxiety disorders back to one particular source. Even if this is achieved, the individual may then know the reason for the disorder, but may still have the problem. That is to say, understanding the underlying cause of an anxiety state alone does not guarantee that the conditioned fear reactions and anxiety 'habit' which will have been reinforced with time, will magically disappear. Such areas can require specific work. If, however, after working on yourself for some time you still seem no nearer to controlling anxiety, it may be that possible underlying reasons for your behaviour will need to be addressed.

THE RELEVANCE OF A PSYCHOLOGICAL APPROACH FOR POSITIVE CHANGE

Coryell and Winkur (1991) note how 'normal' anxiety can be seen to have three main components: 1) cognitive processes (thoughts), 2) physiological arousal, and 3) coping strategies. One or more of these components become abnormal in an individual suffering with an anxiety state. As we have seen, such abnormalities can include those outlined in figure 5.

It is appropriate that a programme of management of anxiety disorders includes a means of addressing all such abnormalities in the anxiety response. Choosing psychological treatment as a main approach is particularly

	Abnormal anxiety response	Psychological treatment
Cognitive processes	There can be a preoccupation with negative thoughts, misinterpretation of bodily sensations and catastrophic notions regarding the potential danger of normal everyday circumstances.	Maladaptive thoughts which can be responsible for triggering subsequent 'anxiety symptoms' and relapse can be greatly remedied with the help of *cognitive therapy* (working in a positive manner with such thoughts).
Physiological arousal	Arousal can become excessive, developing into a panic attack for some individuals. (This can involve such symptoms as accelerated heart rate, tension of muscles, increased perspiration and change in the breathing pattern.)	*Relaxation and self-hypnosis* techniques can be useful tools when wishing to help reduce physiological arousal.
Coping strategies	There can be a reliance on avoidance behaviour resulting in an individual missing out on the chance to decondition the anxiety response and reappraise the true level of danger in any situation.	*Cognitive therapy, relaxation and self-hypnosis* can also become important allies when working towards the more positive coping strategy of approaching and confronting anxiety situations.

Figure 5   Psychological treatment for abnormalities in the anxiety response

suitable as it can satisfy this criterion. (Figure 5 dis, the psychological approaches which constitute the man, focus of this book, and the abnormal anxiety responses which they can benefit.) As well as being capable of directly addressing abnormalities in the anxiety response, a psychological approach can also work that bit deeper; facilitating when appropriate the uncovering of, and therapeutic work with, possible underlying psychological reasons for such abnormalities.

In Chapter 10 medical treatment presently available for the management of anxiety disorders is outlined. Drug therapy should never be used as a substitute for counselling or psychotherapeutic approaches. Compared to psychological treatment it has many problems, including resistance to medication, the risk of dependence, and concerns of relapse on withdrawal of medication. This has led many experts, including Dr Eriksson *et al* (1990), to advise that drugs are best avoided as a general rule. The 'Drug and Therapeutics Bulletin' (1993), edited by Joe Collier, concludes in the paper, *Psychological treatment for anxiety – an alternative to drugs?*, that: 'Psychological treatments are an effective alternative to drug therapy for patients with acute stress, generalized anxiety disorder, agoraphobia and panic disorders, and in general result in a lower relapse rate once treatment is stopped.'

The good news is that regardless of how vulnerable you are in the face of anxiety, you can learn many ways to help improve and manage your situation. As the old saying goes: 'If you do what you've always done, you'll get what you've always gotten'! This book aims to equip you with new skills that will help you to instigate positive change, and thus allow you to move forward out of the vicious spirals of anxiety. Read on and free yourself!

CHAPTER 3

Paving the Way for Success

One thing is certain in the treatment of anxiety, there are no short-cuts, and the cure takes effort from the sufferer.

Kenneth Hambly

Before you begin practising the ideas laid out in this book it is important to set the scene for success. Many factors can influence the results you will achieve when working on yourself. These include you wanting things to change, having clear goals and realistic expectations, being committed to helping yourself and accepting your situation. We will now explore each of these factors in turn.

WANTING THINGS TO CHANGE

This problem was very frustrating for me. I wanted so much to be 'normal'.

Susan

Before you can change you need to *want* that change. It can be useful to list as many benefits as possible you can obtain as a result of working on yourself. Making yourself fully aware of these can strengthen your motivation and desire to change.

You might think that nobody likes being anxious or afraid, but sometimes it can have its advantages. We don't usually continue acting in a certain way unless we're getting something out of it. Somebody who becomes agoraphobic may, for instance, find that their spouse and everyone around them becomes more attentive; their shopping is done for them, they don't have to go out and earn a living and life's responsibilities are taken on by other people. These benefits or 'secondary gains' can serve to reinforce and maintain the very behaviour and feelings which cause the person aggravation. If the person gives up the anxiety or fear, he or she also loses those benefits resulting from their symptoms.

In some cases changing may also mean facing and dealing with any underlying problems of the symptoms. A mother of a handicapped child, for example, in addition to attending to the special needs of her child, may also have to struggle with a myriad other tasks such as washing, cleaning and shopping. Unless she gets a break every once in a while she may have a problem with physical exhaustion, particularly if she has other children. If she feels overwhelmed and comes to a point where she cannot cope any more her mind may 'help out' by producing the physical symptoms of panic attacks.

The panic attacks can physically stop her and make her take rest and time out for herself. They may also act as a means of getting those around her to give her the attention and help she needs. This shows the protective nature of the mind and how it 'looks out' for us. Sufferers may feel that this is a strange way to view it, but the symptoms can act as a 'friend', rather than being the 'enemy', in the short-term. It is a way of coping until something more appropriate can be sorted out.

It is important that this mother deals with the underlying problem of her reluctance to be assertive and ask for help. She needs to take time to care for herself and her needs as well as for those of her children. Then the benefits of the panic attacks will be satisfied in other healthier, more appropriate, ways. This can result in the attacks no longer being 'required'.

Some people will have very low motivation to change because they are reluctant to let go of the benefits of their symptoms, or because they are unwilling to confront and deal with any possible underlying problems at the root of the symptoms. They will often make only half-hearted attempts to improve things, and the results of their effort will usually strongly reflect this. As noted by Roger and McWilliams (1991): 'If you're not actively involved in getting what you want, you don't really want it.'

Before you read any further, decide you really want to change. To obtain maximum benefit from the techniques in this book you will need to work through the following questions:

- In what way will your life be different and better when you have changed?
- Are you getting any benefits from your present situation? (What has stopped you from changing so far?)
- How could you get these benefits in other more appropriate ways?
- Is there any possible underlying problem you should be confronting and sorting out?

You may find you do not have answers for all these questions at a conscious level. For example, sometimes people may not be consciously aware of any benefits or underlying problems/reasons associated with their behaviour. In Chapter 8 we will explore methods of uncovering such possible information and negotiating with the subconscious mind to your advantage.

HAVING CLEAR GOALS AND REALISTIC EXPECTATIONS

I appreciate in the future I may still experience the occasional twinge of anxiety, but I now know how to deal with it.

Joanne

Rather than dealing with vague notions of the way you would like things to be in your life, it is helpful to be really clear on what you desire for yourself. For example, it can be useful to imagine specific situations, seeing in your mind the way you would like to feel and act and the qualities you would wish to possess. Some people find it helpful to think of a role model who exemplifies the desired behaviour, either someone they know or a person created in their imagination.

It is of vital importance that you check that your goals are realistic. Allowing for no discomfort whatsoever can mean that a slight sign of a symptom may whirl you into panic. Give yourself permission to be human! Allow for flexibility and imperfection in your goals. If you are someone who thinks you should be calm and happy all the time then you may be creating extra distress for yourself. Each of your emotions will have a time and a place in your life; I do not know anyone who escapes bad feelings and who is in control all of the time. No one can be entirely free of problems.

It is also important that your expectation regarding the rate at which you will benefit from working on yourself is realistic, or you will easily become discouraged. There is no such thing as a magic wand that can bring about instant miracle cures. While it is fully understandable that you wish to put an end to your discomfort as soon as possible, concern that things are not working as quickly as you would like only leads to frustration, which in turn can result in more anxiety! Recovery takes time. There are no short-cuts. Allow as much time as is necessary for recovery; see it as open-ended. Setting a time limit may only serve to burden you with further pressures.

Improvement tends to be a gradual process, and may be interspersed with times when little benefit is noticed, or there is even a recurrence of your initial symptoms. It is important to realize that you are continually progressing. Plateaus or setbacks, which are generally only temporary in nature, are a normal and necessary part of the overall process of improvement. Setbacks in particular may be an indication that you have been overdoing things and need to slow down. It will not be long before things will move forward in a positive way once more, provided you continue to work on yourself.

It can be useful to break your main goal of recovery down into a number of steps. For instance, it will be more appropriate for an agoraphobic to aim at feeling comfortable walking to the front gate before moving on to the next goal of feeling happy to walk around the block, and so on. Breaking goals into digestible steps helps to set more reasonable targets, and also provides the opportunity for many intermediate successes along the way. This can help to keep you motivated. It will also be encouraging in time to compare yourself to the way you used to be when things were at their worst. (Such a comparison will prove much more fruitful than the usual tendency to judge yourself in relation to the way you feel you *should* be, or the way other people appear to be.)

BEING COMMITTED TO WORKING ON YOURSELF

No one is to blame for getting into this frame of mind, but you are if you don't do anything about it!

Peter

This book will teach you ways of learning to control anxiety. I hope you will find this learning process enjoyable and interesting, but it is important to realize that to obtain maximum benefit from all you learn you will need to put in time and effort. You are the one who will then make the positive changes happen. The techniques will require regular and consistent practice.

To put in the effort that is required you will need to be committed to your goals, and this commitment will very much depend on how much it is worth to you to achieve and then maintain positive change. Until you are committed there is always the chance to draw back. Remember, people who stay in the middle of the road generally get run over!

ACCEPTING YOUR SITUATION

Because I had always been such a strong person in the past, coping well with whatever life put my way, I became very impatient with myself when I began to suffer with anxiety symptoms. I could not accept that this was happening to me. However, denying I had a problem was not going to make it disappear. Before I could benefit from help I had to accept my situation for what it was.

June

Many people with an anxiety disorder experience feelings of shame. They often deny the problem because they feel the situation is unacceptable. They can frequently become quite impatient with their symptoms, chastising and be-littling themselves for being the way they are. (So often we can be our own worst critic!) For instance, they may think: 'This is really stupid! Other people do not have this problem. I should not be this way!' This can in turn further intensify their anxiety.

Many other sufferers handle their situation by choosing to believe they have a physical illness, which is generally believed to be so much easier to 'fix', and is devoid of the stigma that society still attaches to emotional problems. This too can put barriers in the way of recovery.

This book is about reducing negative feelings. However, strange as it may sound, you probably will not be able to overcome these negative feelings until you first of all accept them. This does not mean you are adopting a defeatist attitude, or condoning such feelings; just that you are allowing yourself to see them for what they are. Learning about what may be happening to you (*see* Chapters 1 and 2) is beneficial in this respect. Demystifying your situation can help you to view your symptoms as valid and normal under the circumstances for what you are dealing with. This can lead to a positive acceptance, which in turn can help you to feel better about yourself.

Accepting your limitations as well as your strengths can in itself be a major step towards recovery. Rather than avoid or deny feelings, you can learn to handle negative emotions by accepting them, which in turn puts you in a better position to cope with them directly in many positive ways. Accept your bad days and celebrate the good ones, which can increase with time.

CHAPTER 4

Taking Responsibility for Yourself and Your Thoughts

Until we make the inner changes, until we are willing to do the mental work, nothing outside of us is going to change. Yet, the inner changes can be so incredibly simple because the only thing we really need to change are our thoughts.

Louise L Hay

What you say to yourself in your thoughts can make a dramatic difference to your quality of life. As noted in Chapter 2, people who suffer with an anxiety disorder are prone to talking to themselves in a negative and worried manner. These thoughts can then trigger feelings of anxiety, fear and panic. This chapter will deal with the very important work of altering such maladaptive thoughts, helping you to make your mind work to your advantage.

YOUR SUBCONSCIOUS MIND

Your mind processes information both consciously and subconsciously. The subconscious mind is that part of your mind of which you are unaware; it is in charge of the autonomic nervous system, controlling all involuntary bodily functions as well as storing all our experiences in the form of memories. The deeper part of your mind is responsible also for your entire range of feelings, beliefs, habits, self-image and intuition. Every conscious thought is said to contribute to the building of the subconscious mind. It's very much the case of 'what you put in is what you get out'. So you need to watch what you think!

BEING YOUR OWN BEST FRIEND

If someone spoke positively to you all the time, the chances are you would feel good in their company and would spend a lot of time with them. Similarly, if a person spoke negatively to you all the time, you would eventually start feeling really bad in their presence and would probably try to get away from them! You can move away from people but you cannot escape from your thoughts. If you allow them to be negative this can lead to negative feelings, attitudes and beliefs. On the other hand, positive thinking can create a sense of well-being and positive expectation.

It makes sense to be your own best friend rather than your own worst enemy. Think of the way you usually talk to yourself when anxious. If it's negative, ask yourself: 'If I had a friend in my situation would I ever speak to them in this negative way? What tempo and tone of voice would I use? What would I say to comfort, reassure and support them?' Now decide to start speaking to yourself in the same respectful and helpful way. It is also important to praise and motivate yourself in your efforts to change.

CHOOSING AND DECIDING HOW YOU ARE GOING TO FEEL

Once you realize that your thoughts create your feelings it becomes clear that although you may not in life be in control of what actually happens to you, you are in charge of your response to these events. Lazarus and Folkman (1984) insist that a person's perception of a situation is the most significant component of stress and anxiety. Someone who says 'that person/situation makes me feel edgy' has forgotten that it's impossible for any person or situation to create or cause feelings in you. Until you interpret things in your thoughts and give them meaning you cannot experience an emotional reaction. Therefore you can decide how you are going to feel at any particular time by choosing how you are going to allow yourself to think and interpret life around you.

People who actively seek out adrenaline-producing activities (such as bungee jumping) are choosing to trigger the 'fight-or-flight' response in their bodies and decide to view the experience of the ensuing sensations as 'excitement'. It could be said that although you are probably unaware of what you are doing, in choosing to think in a negative and anxious manner, you are bringing on similar sensations to those chased by 'thrill seekers' but you are interpreting and labelling them as 'anxiety' or 'panic'!

Since you own your thoughts you can control them. It sounds simple but it gets results – when you change the way you think, you change the way you feel. You can overcome anxiety. No matter what you are faced with there is always something positive you can say to yourself about it.

HOW TO CHANGE NEGATIVE THOUGHTS TO POSITIVE ONES

How do you go about reversing these negative patterns and habits of thought? Firstly, you need to become aware of the way you allow your thoughts to operate. If you can identify negative trends in your thoughts, then you are well on the way to improving things.

Reframing

Every situation has a positive as well as a negative side. If in the past you were only reporting the negative, you were lying to yourself by omission. You were not informing your subconscious mind of the positive aspects or potential of the situation. As previously stated, the meaning of anything depends on how you decide to interpret it. For example, someone might say: 'Last week I made the biggest mistake of my entire life', when they could instead decide to reinterpret or reframe this as: 'Last week I learned some very important lessons!'

Suggesting to yourself what you want rather than what you do not want

So many people allow themselves to worry and think negatively about future events. I remember a client once saying to me that he felt guilty if he did not worry about things; if he did not worry about something he felt he was neglecting it. The reality is that you cannot benefit or control future events by worrying about them. In fact, by thinking in this non-productive way you may actually be helping what you fear most to occur!

For example, the best man at a wedding is encouraging a negative result if he allows himself to think before delivering his speech: 'When I open my mouth to speak I know I'll stutter.' He would help himself to give a clear, well-presented speech if he set things up in a positive way instead, by thinking: 'When I open my mouth I can speak clearly, calmly and with confidence.'

It is also important to keep individual words positive, whenever possible, as well as the meaning of the complete sentence. For example, if someone was to think, 'I am not going to feel stressed and anxious during that meeting tomorrow', it may appear that they are thinking positively. However, if I were to say to you 'Whatever you do, don't think of a pink elephant', what would happen? Some of you would probably find that the image of a pink elephant popped into your mind immediately! This is because to 'not think' of something we first of all often need to think of it! So the example regarding the meeting may in fact place the suggestion of 'stress and anxiety' into the person's mind, regardless of the meaning of the sentence as a whole. It would be more helpful to think about the meeting using positive words, such as: 'I am going to feel "relaxed and calm" during the meeting tomorrow.'

You can bring the very best out of yourself by suggesting in your thoughts what you want, rather than what you do not want. As noted by Mary, a former client: 'I now believe that worry is a wasted emotion. You can feel more in control and make positive changes in your life – if you are taught how to do so.'

Watching yourself as you speak

Just as you can influence your subconscious mind with your thoughts, you can also influence it when you speak aloud. Other people listen when you speak, and so does your subconscious mind. As well as keeping what you say positive, you can ensure your mind does not pick up on negativity in other ways by toning down your vocabulary and speaking normally in a matter-of-fact way. Unless you are going to see a therapist, who would want to ask about your feelings in detail, avoid any melodrama when talking about anxiety.

Not 'trying' when you want to succeed

It is also important to realize that the deeper part of your mind will often take literally the meaning of words you put in there. For example, if you say you are 'trying' to be a calmer person, your subconscious mind will help you to 'try', but not necessarily to 'succeed'! The word 'try' implies a lot of effort but ultimately failure to achieve your goal. Phrases like, 'I am a calmer person' or 'I am becoming a calmer person', will be much more productive in helping you on your way to being more at ease.

DEALING WITH HABITUAL NEGATIVE THOUGHTS

Thinking in a negative way has been a feature in some people's lives for such a long time it has well and truly become a habit. There follow two methods for combating this problem.

The 'Stop' Method

This method not only helps to break habitual negative thinking but also, as you repeatedly practise it, creates the new habit of positive thinking. Remember, anything you repeat often enough can become automatic. Whenever you have a negative thought, think 'Stop', or see a 'Stop' road sign in your mind. Then, dealing directly with the subject matter, change the negative focus of your thoughts into a positive one. Make the very best of reality as it is. (*See* figure 6 for some examples.) If the habit of negative thinking is deeply engrained you will need to do this exercise persistently and aggressively.

Neuro-Linguistic Programming for extra-stubborn habitual negative thoughts

Some of you may find when using the 'Stop' method that there are some negative thoughts that are so deeply entrenched that they jump into your mind before you've even realized it or had a chance to say 'Stop'! It helps to give such thoughts some special attention.

The following technique involves investigating what changes can be made to such a thought to help lessen or neutralize the negative feeling it usually produces. Work is then carried out to store the thought in the mind in a new, more positive, way with these beneficial alterations. This results in the thought not having the power to affect

Negative thought		Positive focus
If I go to the supermarket I will feel more anxious and make my problem worse.	*Stop*	Success is allowing myself to go out and confront that situation. In doing this I am practising and working towards recovery. I am stronger than I know and I can do it! I give myself permission to feel good about myself for having the courage to do this.
Oh no, here it comes again! I feel a panic attack brewing. I feel scared.	*Stop*	I can allow this to pass off in its own way. Breathing slowly and calmly and reassuring myself in my mind that I am 'okay' can help this process. I can feel proud of myself for coping the best way I can.
I might die during a panic attack.	*Stop*	I have had many such episodes in the past and have always survived. They are essentially harmless. I am safe.
This is stupid! No one else is this way. There must be something terrible wrong with me. I must be going insane.	*Stop*	I can accept that these symptoms are normal under the circumstances I am dealing with. I can be a support to myself through this. Like so many others who have overcome this condition I can notice how with my new coping skills and a bit of patience things will improve.

Figure 6 The 'Stop' Method: some examples of how negative thoughts can be turned around into thoughts with a more positive focus

you in the same manner as it did in the past. The method originates from the work of Richard Bandler, one of the founders of what is known as 'Neuro-Linguistic Programming' (NLP). NLP deals with the way we structure our subjective experience in our minds. (We will be exploring some other useful NLP techniques in Chapters 5, 7 and 8.)

When working with this technique give yourself 10 to 15 minutes free of any interruptions. As with many of the exercises in this book, you may find it useful to record the structure of the exercise on a tape. Use a soft voice tone and leave pauses where appropriate so that you can play back the tape to guide yourself through the technique. Alternatively, you may wish to memorize the exercise, or ask someone to read the structure to you until you have become more familiar with it.

Exercise

1 Focus on a frequently recurring negative thought which leaves you feeling bad. For example: 'I'm going to have a panic attack.'

2 Sit down with your eyes closed and hear that thought in your mind the way you usually do. Note whatever negative feeling it produces in you. Open your eyes and get ready for a bit of experimentation with that sentence.

3 By making various alterations to that thought, you can test which ones lessen or neutralize the negative feeling produced. Close your eyes once more. Think of the *speed* of the thought. If, for example, it is fast and urgent, test slowing the thought right down, almost like a record on at the wrong speed – annoyingly slow! Note whether the feeling after the thought has changed as a result. Open your eyes. If the feeling has improved take a note of this alteration.

4 Put the thought back to its usual speed, and get ready for the next test.

5 Experiment in a similar way by altering the *voice* in your head which is speaking the thought (presumably your own voice). Replace it with that of a cartoon character, or someone you find particularly amusing. Once you have

opened your eyes note if this alteration has helped to lessen or neutralize the negative feeling.

6 Put the thought back to 'your usual' before doing the final test. Imagine your favourite song or piece of *music* in the background as you hear the thought. This is a bit like doing mental acrobatics! Remember, however, that the 'way' you do it isn't what is important; the effect the alteration has on the negative feeling is what is of interest. Open your eyes and, as with all alterations, only take note of it if you find things improved.

7 Now it's time to put together what you have learned. Amalgamate any alterations you noted as improving the feeling, and hear that thought in your mind in this new way. For example, you may have Donald Duck saying the words very slowly with 'Jingle Bells' being sung in the background! If none of the alterations I have mentioned help, create some of your own. (For further information on other possible 'alterations' you can make, read Richard Bandler's book *Using Your Brain For A Change*.)

8 Once you are happy that the negative feeling from the thought is improved or neutralized through the use of this method, reinforce the thought with these new associations. Your subconscious can assimilate the new process by you rehearsing the thought with these alterations five times with your eyes closed (it helps to count on your fingers as your mind has enough to occupy it already!).

9 Now try to get the thought the 'old' way as easily as you could to begin with. The chances are you will have to work a bit at 'keeping out' the alterations your mind now associates with the thought. This means it is no longer automatic or habitual the 'old' way. It's now stored in the deeper part of your mind in this new, more positive, way. So if at any time in the future that thought pops into your mind before you can say 'Stop', you can be sure that it will not have the same effect as it did in the past. This has to be good news!

In my experience, a lot of people find that once this technique has been completed they no longer take any notice of the thought which used to cause them so much trouble.

It no longer produces a negative feeling. I do recall one client, however, who came to me seeking help to become a non-smoker. Much to her amusement, she found that many months afterwards she would still hear in her mind her favourite tune and the cartoon character 'Mr McGoo' saying: 'I need a cigarette!!' Because the craving this thought used to produce had completely disappeared, she just chuckled to herself twenty times a day instead of smoking her usual 20 cigarettes!

USING CUE CARDS

Some people find it very helpful to surround themselves with cue cards containing positive phrases or effective quotes. They put them on mirrors, their desk, in their diary, in the car, on the refrigerator door, and so on.

If you are particularly anxious in a certain situation, why not make a cue card specific to that situation? You could bring it with you to read and to help yourself through that time, until your mind becomes more spontaneous in its creation of appropriate positive thoughts.

A WORD OF WARNING: OLD BELIEFS WILL NEED SOME TIME TO CHANGE

To begin with you may find yourself putting in positive thoughts you do not fully believe. This should not surprise you since your old, often negative, beliefs will probably dominate your subconscious mind at first. Once your mind has heard the new positive thoughts often enough to create a strong reserve, the new more positive outlook can predominate in the deeper part of your mind.

Persistence with positive thoughts is the key. Repetition is important. The more positive thoughts you put into your mind the better. You don't need to wait for an opportunity to do the 'stop' method before relaying positive messages to the deeper part of your mind. Set areas of your life up in a positive way; every chance you get, put in a positive thought! For example, as you look in the mirror each morning, talk positively to your reflection about yourself and the day ahead. (If you are living with someone it may be wise to explain why you are doing this!) Once your beliefs start to alter, your goals of positive change can seem that much more attainable.

CHAPTER 5

Using your Imagination

The mind is its own place, and in itself can make heaven of hell, a hell of heaven.

John Milton

In addition to working in a positive way with your 'self talk', your imagination can also be used in many ways to your advantage to help combat anxiety. In particular the use of imagery can be a very powerful means of working on yourself, since any one image can literally be worth hundreds of verbal suggestions.

In this chapter a range of visualization techniques will be explored. Choose those which seem most appropriate to your own circumstances for everyday use.

POSITIVE VISUALIZATION

If you were strolling around an art gallery, certain pictures might leave you with an unpleasant feeling inside (for example, a bloody battlefield scene), whereas looking at others (such as a beautiful beach scene) might help you to feel at ease. 'Pictures' or 'ideas' you sense in your mind's eye can work in a similar way.

Since what you perceive in your mind affects how you feel, this can be used as another tool to your advantage. If you are preoccupied with frightening fantasies, or daydreams which make you anxious, you can decide to focus instead on pleasant, peaceful scenes, such as an image of a place you love, or images of a holiday you really enjoyed. In so doing you can alter your feelings in a positive way. Some people have such a good imagination they can almost feel that they are actually in these beautiful places or memories. A poor imagination can be trained and developed with practise.

Dr Vernon Coleman (1993) recommends the following to help improve your quality of life. Write as many happy memories as you can think of in a notebook. (If you cannot think of any, make them up!) Choose your favourite seven and relive them in detail. Remember and re-experience the pleasant feelings associated with those times. Allow yourself to become absorbed in these memories first thing in the morning and last thing at night, or whenever you wish to lift your mood.

Alternatively you could work with fear and feelings of anxiety in a more active, direct manner. There follow some ideas of how you might do this. You may wish to:

- Imagine your anxiety drifting away from your body and mind into a large, white cloud in the sky. The more anxiety that cloud absorbs from you, the darker it can become. With a sense of deep relief watch as that black, 'laden down' cloud drifts further away from you, until it is out of sight.
- Write your fears on an imaginary piece of paper which you can then throw into a fire and watch burn away.
- Visualize dumping frightening fantasies and anxious feelings into a rubbish skip, and walking away feeling calmer and more at ease.
- In your mind, see your body being filled with a healing, peaceful, golden light. Allow it to reach out and touch every part of you.
- Imagine your body is that of a strong healthy tree. Notice how the leaves seem to dance in the breeze in a carefree way. The roots of the tree are deep in the

ground holding you safe and steady. This can give you a sense of inner security as you continue to branch out further in your life.

Take time to invent and experiment with imagery of your own. Be creative! Positive visualization exercises, coupled with positive self-talk, can really help to improve your mood and reduce anxiety in a profound way.

MENTAL REHEARSAL

As strange as it may initially seem, a lot of the time we get what we expect from life. As was discussed in the last chapter, if you set things up in a positive way in your mind you help yourself achieve a positive outcome. Setting things up negatively can mean you actually attract what you fear. Many people curious about why their worst fears always seem to happen have probably spent most of their lives thinking in a frightened manner about what they fear most!!

Using your imagination in a positive way can help to improve your 'performance' in every field. Prather (1973) found that trainee pilots using mental practice of manoeuvres for landing aircraft were rated better in their landing skill proficiency than trainees who did not use this method. This demonstrates how practising in your imagination can produce outstanding results.

You can do this too by practising the way you would like to be in any area of your life. Visualize the situation the very best way it could realistically be. If, for example, you have a social phobia, imagine feeling really happy when you get an invitation to go out, and enjoying the night out and finding people's conversation interesting. The stronger you can experience those positive feelings, the stronger the motivation to go for that goal.

If you find it difficult to create those feelings, it may help to cast your mind back to a night out you enjoyed before you developed your phobia, and dwell on how good you were able to feel then. Alternatively, as recommended in Chapter 3, you may choose a role model who exemplifies the desired qualities, feelings and behaviour. Just as a talented actor can assume the characteristics of the person he or she is playing, you can 'pretend' to be your role model in a social situation and notice how your feelings of confidence can increase.

Imagining in this way over and over again will impress a positive attitude about social situations on your subconscious mind, and can help to override any past negative beliefs. This can subsequently have a positive effect on your feelings and behaviour. If you have a special event to work towards, I would recommend daily reinforcement of the positive imagery for at least a week beforehand.

POSITIVE FORWARD PROJECTION

You can take this positive imagining even further by projecting yourself forward in your mind to a point where you have long overcome uncomfortable levels of anxiety. Imagine embarking on a journey into the future that takes you to a time when your anxiety is under control. As you find yourself there, look back into the past and wonder how you ever allowed yourself to be so anxious for so long!

Look back in time and see how you worked on things step-by-step, how you overcame any obstacles and progressed towards the point where you are now. As you travel back to the present, you can feel good about having such a positive map in your mind as a guide for the future. To get somewhere, it always helps to know where you want to go; if you have a map as well it makes the journey so much easier!

THE 'SWISH' TECHNIQUE

It is clear that we often give the deeper part of our mind confusing signals when it comes to what we want for ourselves. The following NLP technique created by Bandler (1985) uses imagery to help clarify further for your subconscious mind what you want and what you do not want. It also aids the process of reprogramming your predominant thoughts in a more positive direction. This is particularly useful as usually we tend to gravitate towards our predominant thoughts. When you direct your mind in a positive way, you will notice how often your feelings and behaviour will have a very strong tendency to go in the same direction.

At this stage it is important once again to set aside some time for yourself. Sit in a comfortable chair in a quiet room. I have laid out the 'swish' technique in a step-by-step, easy-to-follow progression.

Exercise
1 Make yourself comfortable and close your eyes.
2 Visualize a screen in your mind, as if you are at the cinema. Now see an image of yourself the way you **do not want to be** on this screen. For example, it might be a picture of you looking stressed at work. Make this picture as unpleasant as it can be. Feel the feelings that come with looking at that image.
3 Now wipe this 'negative' image away from the screen, and see on the screen an image of the way **you want to be**. Make it as pleasant and as attractive as possible. For example, it might be you looking calm and 'on top of things' at work. Step into that image in your mind and stay there until you can feel how good it is. Enjoy feeling calm and in control. Take time to explore this before wiping that positive image off the screen, leaving it blank once more.
4 Now see the 'negative' picture big and bright on the screen. Put a small, dark image of the 'positive' picture, stuck on like a stamp in the wrong place on a postcard, in the lower right-hand corner (*see* figure 7a).

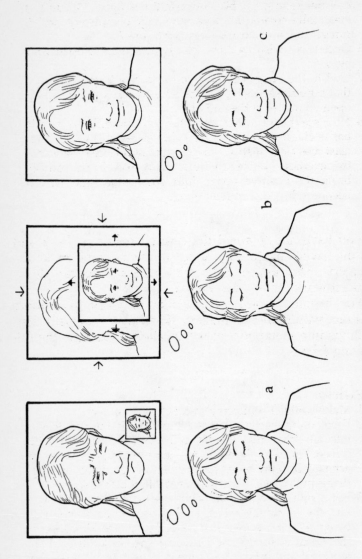

Figure 7 The 'swish' technique

5 As fast as you can say 'swish' allow the small dark positive image to grow big and bright (*see* figure 7b) until it eventually covers the negative image completely, which can get dim and shrink away (*see* figure 7c).

6 Once this 'swish' is done, blank the screen or open your eyes.

7 'Swish' the images about five times. See if you can do it that bit quicker each time. Be sure to blank the screen or open your eyes at the end of each 'swish'.

8 Now see the 'negative' image in your mind. If the 'swish' has been effective this image should be hard to get or at least less clear than it was in your mind before you did this exercise. Notice now how easily and clearly you can bring the positive image into your mind, and how it becomes the predominant image.

If you have not obtained the desired result, go back and do the 'swish' again. Figure out how you could make the imagery more appropriate or what else you can do to make it work for you. Be creative.

For instance, some people like to work in a more abstract way with the imagery. They may represent their feelings in a metaphorical way. Take for example the following exercise:

Exercise

1 Make yourself comfortable and close your eyes.

2 Focus on the feeling you want to change. Put that feeling into an image that directly represents it visually on the screen. For example, a knotted, tense feeling in your stomach may be represented by an image of tight knots in a rope that is pulled taut. Now wipe that image off the screen.

3 Focus on the feeling you want to achieve. Work in a similar way to the above. A feeling of calmness and well-being may be represented visually by a modification of the 'negative image'. In the case above the knots could be loosened or untied, the rope allowed to be more lax. Alternatively, a completely new positive image, such as a calm ocean scene representing the calmer feeling, may be

chosen and placed on the screen. This can then be 'swished' in place of the negative image in your mind. Ensure that whatever image you choose calms you as you view it in your mind.

I remember using this technique with a client whose anxiety about sex was causing her pelvic muscles around the vagina to contract each time intercourse was attempted (vaginismus). When she came to see me she was beginning to avoid sex whenever possible.

I asked this lady to visualize this feeling of contraction. She imagined an elastic band pulled as tightly as possible without breaking. As she viewed this image in her mind I asked her to rate the tension she could feel at that moment in her pelvic muscles. She reported a score of 8/10 on a 'tension scale', 10/10 being the strongest tension she had ever experienced there.

She had produced this tension herself, and so she also had the power to get rid of it. In her case to achieve the feeling she wanted (a relaxation of the pelvic muscles), all she had to do was manipulate in a positive manner in her mind the elastic band image, rather than 'swish' in a completely new image. She visualized the elastic band being released and falling lax. Within about 20 seconds she reported her pelvic muscles relaxing to 0/10 on the 'tension scale'.

This was a skill she could use in the future to help her to 'let go' and relax. The approach, combined with other work we engaged in, allowed her to feel much more comfortable about sexual encounters.

SETTING UP A CALM ANCHOR

Did you know that you can 'anchor' feelings to a specific spot on your body? Once this anchor is established you can recall and sometimes relive the feelings by pressing that spot on your body which serves as a trigger for these feelings. This simple technique merely uses the mind's natural talent for linking things together and making associations (see the section 'Anxiety as a learned response', Chapter 2).

The process of making associations usually happens without our conscious awareness. It is an everyday occurrence. For instance, if you were to hear a song that you used to listen to ten years ago, it could automatically trigger off a flood of memories about what you were experiencing at that time. If you are driving and see a red light you immediately associate that with stopping. The following exercise, which should only take 5 to 10 minutes, shows how you can use associations to set up your very own calm anchor.

Exercise
1 Allow yourself to feel comfortable with your eyes closed. Think of a time in your life when you felt really calm and relaxed, such as when you were enjoying a favourite holiday.
2 Imagine yourself in that place. Immerse yourself in that experience, making it as real as possible by exploring that place with all your senses: see what you see there, hear what you hear, notice any characteristic smells of that place, touch your surroundings in your imagination. Use your sense of taste if appropriate. Allow your breathing to become slow and deep.
3 When you can feel the relaxation of that experience in your body and mind, anchor it to a certain part of your body; for instance, some people will bring a finger to meet their thumb. Hold that anchor long enough to allow the association between that touch and the relaxed feelings to occur (usually about 20 seconds), then release the anchor.
4 Test the anchor. If you wish you can strengthen the association with repetition, using the same experience or setting up other relaxing and calming experiences in the same way in your mind, and anchoring these good feelings to the same spot.

Once the anchor is established, anytime you feel anxious, touch the spot in the same way with the same pressure and notice how you can recall or relive the pleasant relaxing and calming feelings. As with any coping technique, it is best to use it early in the development of discomfort, before the anxiety becomes a runaway reaction. You now have the security of knowing you carry a calm anchor with you at all times!

CHAPTER 6

Relaxation and Self-hypnosis

It is important from time to time to slow down, to go away by yourself, and simply 'Be'.

Eileen Caddy

This chapter is broken down into three main sections. Firstly we will explore some methods of relaxed breathing and a technique for relaxation of the entire body; then comes a section giving some background on hypnosis; and finally we look at the area of self-hypnosis in some detail.

RELAXATION

Many people suffering with an anxiety disorder can be uncomfortable with the notion of relaxation, believing that it is important to be always alert and on the look out for danger. However, the reality of the situation is very different. Just as it would be inappropriate to be constantly relaxed, so too it is undesirable to be continuously anxious. Achieving the right balance is all important. Paradoxically, learning to let go a little more can ultimately put you more in control of your situation!

The benefits of relaxation are many. Once people have learned to relax they often report such changes as better sleeping habits and a general feeling of calm and ease. Kabat-Zinn *et al* (1992) found in their study that a training programme based on stress reduction and relaxation effectively reduced symptoms of anxiety and panic, and helped to maintain this state in patients with generalized anxiety disorder, panic disorder or panic disorder with agoraphobia.

Methods of relaxed breathing

Some people find that they breathe very quickly (hyperventilate) when anxious. This washes out the carbon dioxide in the blood and can lead to such symptoms as tingling in the fingers, painful contractions of the hands and feet, dizziness and fainting. An easy way to solve this problem is to continue breathing deeply, but with a paper bag held over the mouth so that exhaled carbon dioxide is breathed in again. This helps to regulate the carbon dioxide levels in the blood which consequently relieves the symptoms and helps the sufferer to feel calmer. Ultimately the breathing slows down to a comfortable pace once more. So if this happens to you when anxious, keep a paper bag handy in your pocket!

Other people can suffer a different kind of breathing problem – they find it difficult to catch their breath or breathe deeply. They will find the following breathing exercises useful. Controlling the breath can change your emotional state from negative to neutral or positive. It is very difficult to succumb to unpleasant emotions while breathing deeply and slowly. So if you are feeling anxious and nothing else seems to help, take some slow, deep breaths. Beta Jencks (1990) has outlined many different ways to relax the breathing, including some of the following methods:

Long breath Keeping your shoulders still, imagine inhaling through the fingertips, up the arms and into the shoulders, and then exhaling down the trunk into the abdomen and legs and out of the toes. Repeat.

Breathing through the skin   Imagine inhaling and exhaling through the skin on any part of your body. On each inhalation allow the skin to feel refreshed and invigorated. On each exhalation permit the skin to relax.

Abdominal breathing   Place your hands over the area around your navel and focus your attention there. (According to Taoist philosophy this area is the seat of 'Chi', the body's centre of energy.) Begin inhaling deeply, expanding your stomach as much as possible so that your hands rise gently. Now exhale, taking twice as long as you did to inhale, pulling your abdomen muscles in and noticing the fall of the hands. Repeat.

Filling and emptying a bottle   When liquid is poured into a bottle, the bottom fills before the middle and the top. When the liquid is poured out, the bottom will empty before the top. Imagine that your trunk is a bottle, and fill it with inhaled air from the bottom up. Then allow it to empty in the same manner, first the lower abdomen, then the upper and finally the chest. Repeat no more than three times before resuming normal breathing.

Imagined drug   As you breathe, imagine you are inhaling a bronchodilator agent which relaxes and widens the walls of the air paths in the bronchi and lungs, allowing the air to stream in easily. As you exhale notice the soft collapse of these air passages. Repeat.

Stone into the well   Imagine a deep well in your abdomen. As you breathe imagine that you are following a dropped stone as it falls down the well during each exhalation.

Waves or tides   Lie on your back, and for two or three respiratory cycles imagine your breath is flowing with ocean waves or tides. Feel the passive flowing in and out.

Progressive body relaxation

Dr Edmund Jacobson (1939, 1974), who developed progressive relaxation, noted how difficult it is for an anxious mind to exist within a relaxed body. Progressive relaxation is a very practical technique for releasing tension in your muscles and, as the name suggests, it involves relaxing your body gradually and in individual steps. Put aside a minimum of 20 minutes to really enjoy the following exercise.

Exercise
1 Sit or lie down somewhere comfortable where you feel you will not be disturbed. Close your eyes.
2 Slowly tense the muscles of your feet and hold this tension for a moment. Now let the tension go very gradually.
3 Continue this flexing and relaxing, working upwards through the muscle groups of the body: calves, thighs, buttocks, stomach, chest, back, hands, arms, shoulders, neck and face. As you work through the muscles you may wish to picture in your mind's eye each area letting go, seeing the muscles and tissues relaxing.
4 Enjoy the sense of comfort and relaxation that follows.

Be patient and practise. Gaining confidence with the technique will allow you to relax anywhere, whenever you need to release tension.

HYPNOSIS

Much of what people believe about hypnosis is untrue, including the idea that its prime function is to entertain. In recent years hypnotherapy (therapy experienced in the hypnotic state) has gained considerable respectability in the medical profession for its therapeutic role in the management of many conditions, including those that are stress- and anxiety-related. In previous writing I have explored the area of hypnosis in some depth, and some of that work is included here. If you are interested in learning more about hypnosis I refer you to my book *Health Essentials: Self-Hypnosis. Effective Techniques for Everyday Problems.*

It is difficult to define precisely the nature of hypnosis. For our purposes the best way we can view it is as a state of intense physical and mental relaxation where the subject, although aware of immediate reality, experiences a sense of detachment from it. The focus of attention is usually internal and narrower than when fully alert. Although most people have a natural ability to enter into hypnosis to some degree, unhypnotizable people can include severely disturbed or psychotic individuals, and the mentally handicapped.

A trance is not strange or mysterious. It is a perfectly normal ability, similar to a daydream or the drifting experienced just before falling asleep. You may often experience hypnosis without realizing it; for example, when driving a car you may arrive at your destination unable to remember everything about the journey. Somewhere along the way your conscious mind drifted off, absorbed in your thoughts, leaving the driving of the car and your safety in the care of your subconscious mind. It can also be experienced when you become so engrossed in something (for instance, a book, a television programme, visualization or relaxation exercises) that you lose sense of time and forget where you are.

The similarities between familiar everyday trances and formal hypnosis can often lead people to believe that they have not been in hypnosis because they have expected the experience to be unique or somehow dramatic. When they have not been 'put under', with their surroundings 'blanked out', they feel disappointed. Such unfounded beliefs and expectations about hypnosis often stem from its use in entertainment, and its inaccurate depiction in novels and films. For our purposes the main distinction between everyday trances and formal hypnosis is that the latter involves utilization of the hypnotic state and the power of suggestion with specific results or goals in mind.

In Chapter 4 we explored the notion of the mind processing information both consciously and subconsciously. When fully alert the conscious mind tends to be very critical and often inclined to over-analyse when problem-solving. This can often lead to unproductive results such as avoidance and indecision, refusal to take action and excessive anxiety. The difference between practising self-hypnosis and using the self-talk and visualization techniques described earlier is that the former involves less conscious participation. With the frequently unhelpful conscious mind less likely to interfere, the subject is partially freed from normal logic, enabling the subconscious mind to become more attentive and receptive to therapy in the form of suggestions and imagery.

Instruments that measure the brain's activity have clearly demonstrated a difference in electroencephalograph (EEG) patterns between sleep and hypnosis. When you are in hypnosis you are somewhere in between being fully alert and asleep. The deeper into hypnosis you go, the closer you drift to the state of sleep. In a light state you are nearer to full alertness. Because you are not asleep you will for the most part remain aware of your surroundings and remember everything about the experience. Amnesia, other than 'normal forgetting', will usually only occur if suggestions to this effect have been given to you.

Contrary to myths about hypnosis, when in a trance you stay in control (you will not do anything you do not want to do). Only suggestions that fall within your fundamental interests will be followed through into actual experience. However, even when not in hypnosis, we can sometimes be fooled or tricked by persuasive people into doing something that is not really to our benefit. In theory the same could happen in the presence of an unscrupulous hypnotist. Therefore it is sensible never to allow an unqualified person to use hypnosis with you.

Obviously, this is irrelevant when you are using self-hypnosis, where you are both hypnotist and subject, guiding yourself into the hypnotic state and choosing your own positive suggestions. As you incorporate the practise of self-hypnosis into your everyday routine you too can learn how hypnosis, rather than being a process of taking control of people, is a means of empowering individuals, thereby helping them to feel more in command of their own lives.

SELF-HYPNOSIS

Self-hypnosis has a similar effect to meditation in that it stimulates the right side of the brain, the part responsible for inward awareness, passiveness, feelings of calm and peace and drifting sensations. When practising self-hypnosis it is important not to 'try' to relax. The person who tries to sleep at night is usually the one who stays up all night reading a book! Just allow yourself to relax in your own way at your own pace, to whatever level feels comfortable.

It's important to realize that very good work can be done on most areas in light trance states, and therefore time spent being obsessed with achieving deep states could be spent much more productively. As time moves on you will probably find that sometimes you naturally drift into deeper states anyway. Self-hypnosis, like any other skill, improves and becomes easier with practise. Whether or not you enter deep states of hypnosis is not important; it will be more productive for you to focus on what you want to achieve from utilizing the state to your advantage, whatever level of trance you experience. Above all else, your motivation and desire to effect positive change are most important.

Therapy through the use of imagery and words

Chapter 5 of this book has already given you some ideas on how to use imagery in a therapeutic way through the use of visualization techniques. Practising and developing your visual sense in your imagination can also help to enrich your experience of self-hypnosis. Imagery is often claimed to be the language of the subconscious mind and it is a very powerful method of working on yourself, whether fully alert or practising self-hypnosis.

Some time was spent in Chapter 4 examining the structuring of self-talk suggestions to ensure they can work in the most positive way possible. Obviously the same rules apply when giving yourself suggestions in the hypnotic state, and there are various ways of doing this when practising self-hypnosis. Decide which way you prefer.

1 *Self-talk* This involves simply repeating your suggestions to yourself in your mind when practising your self-hypnosis. However, some people find that as they achieve deeper trance states their conscious mind can become so relaxed and 'drifty' that it can be a bit of an effort to put in the suggestions! The following two ways of giving yourself suggestions overcome this problem.

2 *Written suggestions* This involves writing out your suggestions before you begin your self-hypnosis, reading them about ten times so that your mind is familiar with them and then saying to yourself something like the following: 'As I do my self-hypnosis I want you my subconscious mind to reinforce these suggestions and help to make them become a reality for me in my life in an appropriate way…' Then you follow this with your self-hypnosis, secure in the knowledge that even though your conscious mind may become quite 'drifty', the suggestions of your choice can be worked on at that deeper level of your mind. In effect you have pre-programmed your subconscious mind to work on the suggestions for you while you do your self-hypnosis.

3 *Make a tape* You often see self-hypnosis tapes for sale, many of which are very good. However, these tapes out of necessity tend to be rather general so that they will be flexible enough to cater for a wide audience. Nobody knows better than you (and your therapist if you are working with one) what you want to work on and achieve.

You could therefore make your own individual tape, specifically tailored to meet your personal goals. A full structure for self-hypnosis follows shortly in this chapter which you could read aloud into a tape recorder, including suggestions you feel are important to you. Soft background music can also be added if you feel this will make your self-hypnosis session more enjoyable. Then whenever you wish to take time out to do self-hypnosis all you have to do is put on your self-hypnosis tape, 'drift away' consciously and allow your subconscious mind to do the work!

Precautions and practical considerations

Because hypnosis is a naturally occurring state there are no associated negative side-effects, unlike with the use of certain medications. In fact, once suggestions are kept positive, the only probable side-effects you can expect to experience will be constructive changes in whatever area of your life you are choosing to work on! However, it is still appropriate to take certain precautions when using hypnosis:

1 Avoid self-hypnosis and hypnotherapy if you have a history of epilepsy. There is a slim chance the altered state of hypnosis might induce a fit.
2 Never practise self-hypnosis while involved in any activity that requires you to be alert, such as driving. If you drive after a self-hypnosis session always make sure you are feeling fully back to 'normal' before you sit behind the wheel.

To make your self-hypnosis session as enjoyable as possible choose a place where you can feel both comfortable and safe. Ensure that you will not be disturbed; for example, take the phone off the hook and let those around you know that you wish to have some special time for yourself. If a certain amount of outside noise and distractions are unavoidable, it may help to listen to soothing music through headphones. Rather than attempting to ignore any noises that still filter through you can decide to use them to your advantage. For example, you could link positive suggestions for relaxation to these noises in the following way: 'As I hear the children's laughter I too can feel carefree.' Acknowledging and positively utilizing noises in this way can allow them in time to fade into the background.

Unless you wish to use self-hypnosis to help you to sleep it is best to practise sitting in a comfortable chair rather than lying on a bed. Remember your goal is to be somewhere between being asleep and awake, not actually asleep. You can control the length of time you spend in hypnosis by either setting an alarm clock or giving yourself a simple suggestion beforehand such as: 'I will open my eyes in 20 minutes.' You may be pleasantly surprised at how accurately the latter can work!

It is appropriate, particularly to begin with, to practise self-hypnosis daily for 20 minutes to half-an-hour. Find a way of integrating it into your lifestyle. The right time of the day for your self-hypnosis will very much depend on your schedule. However, make sure you put aside quality time for this important work.

A structure for self-hypnosis

The following exercise shows you one possible structure for self-hypnosis. It is flexible and can be tailored to your specific requirements as you see fit. Be creative with your suggestions and use of imagery (*see* Chapters 4 and 5).

Exercise
1 Sit down and make yourself comfortable. Close your eyes. In your mind give yourself permission to take this precious piece of time just for yourself to be used for your benefit.

2 Focus on your breathing. Allow yourself to become aware of all the different sensations as you breathe. This will include the rise and fall of the ribcage and the breath being a little bit cooler as you breathe in, a little bit warmer as you breathe out. Becoming absorbed in the gentle rhythm of your breathing in time can become quite soothing. Allow your breath to slow down to a comfortable even pace in its own way and time.

3 Notice any tensions in your body or mind and allow them to leave you as you breathe OUT. As you breathe out more and more, any tensions inside can become less and less as you cleanse your body of tensions in this very special way.

4 As you breathe IN, allow comfort and calm to enter your body. Over time as you breathe tensions out of your body, and comfort and calm into your body, you can just allow yourself to breathe into calmness and peace. Give permission for every muscle, nerve and fibre of your body to ease out and relax. (If you wish you may incorporate into this relaxation the methods of relaxed breathing and progressive body relaxation described earlier). Encourage the comfort in the most relaxed part of you to gently sweep and spread throughout your body as time passes by.

5 See five steps in your mind leading down to a special relaxing place of your choice. For instance, you may see a beach, a garden or a forest. As you take each step allow yourself to become more relaxed inside. Count yourself down the steps, 1 to 5, on each or every second breath out (exhalation). This can have the effect of calming and steadying the breathing further.

6 Once in that special place use all your senses to explore it in your mind. Make it seem as real as possible; see what you see there, hear the sounds you might hear in such a place, breathe in the smell of the air, and so on. Really enjoy that beautiful place in your mind.

7 Sit down somewhere very comfortable in your mind and work on your goals of positive change using suggestions and imagery of your choosing.

8 Come back up the steps. Count yourself from 5 back to 1

on each breath in (inhalations), which can help you to become more alert.

9 Last suggestion before opening your eyes: 'When I open my eyes I can feel refreshed, calm and alert.'

10 Open your eyes. Notice how wonderful you can feel! Have a good stretch!

CHAPTER 7

Confronting Anxiety

The only way to get rid of the fear of doing something is to go out and do it. Feel the fear … and do it anyway.

Susan Jeffers

As noted in Chapter 2, particularly in the case of phobic anxiety disorders, it may be that for some people an unpleasant, frightening or traumatic event is associated with the onset of the phobia. The memory of this event can continue to adversely affect them in their present lives. In this chapter we will investigate how you can face and combat the negative emotions associated with such a past memory. This will be followed by a practical exploration of ways you can then set about confronting the situation or object of your fear in the present.

LESSENING OR NEUTRALIZING NEGATIVE FEELINGS ASSOCIATED WITH A PAST MEMORY

A lot of us have negative memories which bother us from time to time, but which do not greatly interfere with our lives. For some people, however, certain bad memories can influence their present and future in a very disruptive way.

A client overcame a phobia of writing in public which appeared to stem from a memory of her school days where a teacher shouted at her so loudly that her hand shook violently as she tried to write. The other children saw this and she felt very embarrassed. As an adult she found that whenever she had to write in public (for example, at the bank) this memory would flood into her mind and her hand would start shaking, thereby creating yet another embarrassing situation. By the time she came to see me she felt it was best to avoid writing in public altogether. Whether you have a memory that bothers you only slightly, or one that has as debilitating an effect as this one, you should be able to find a technique in this section that can help you.

The past is over and done with. The only way it exists is the way we choose to remember it in our minds. This is good news, since we can change memories and their effects. Some of you may be wondering whether it is wise to 'tamper' with beliefs you've gleaned from experience which has helped you with life decision-making. However, memories are notoriously unreliable.

What is a memory? A memory is merely a record of the last time you remembered that memory. We are all aware of how memories can become distorted and inaccurate over time. Also, when the memory was being formed initially it was only an interpretation of the situation at hand. It is reasonable to ask whether it is right to put an inflexible programme into your mind to govern the rest of your life on the basis of one memory which was formed in this fashion.

In order to ensure that any valuable lessons learned in the past are preserved, it can sometimes be more appropriate to modify memories in such a way to reduce or neutralize the associated negative feelings, rather than delete them completely from our minds. Also, with these techniques we wish to work on irrational fears and anxieties only. It may not be wise, for example, for a person who has the memory of being bitten by a dog to change the feeling of appropriate caution they now experience when in the presence of dogs. This is a rational feeling to have. It does not disrupt the person's life, and can serve to protect that person in the future.

Working with a memory generating feelings which are not too intense or traumatic

The following exercise an adaptation of an NLP technique known as 'changing personal history'. It provides a useful means of working with a memory when the negative feelings generated by such a memory are not too intense or traumatic. (Methods for dealing with memories triggering more severe emotions will be outlined after this exercise.) Depending on the type of memory you wish to work on you may feel more comfortable practising this technique in the presence of a supportive friend, or with the help of an experienced NLP therapist.

Exercise
1 Make yourself comfortable and close your eyes.
2 Identify the feeling you wish to work on (such as anxiety, fear or embarrassment).
3 Allow yourself to think back to your earliest memory of experiencing such a feeling.
4 On a 'bad feelings' scale ranging from 1 to 10 (10/10 being the most negative feeling you could experience), think of the number that represents how bad you feel as you remember this incident.
5 Choose a personal resource you would have found useful in that situation in the past (for instance confidence, assertiveness or a sense of calm).
6 Set up an anchor (*see* Chapter 5) for this resource and test this positive anchor.
7 Triggering this anchor allow yourself to travel in your mind once more to the memory you wish to work with. From a dissociated perspective (outside looking in) watch how you would have reacted differently with this useful new resource.

8 Now become associated in that memory (step into it) with this resource and work through the experience in your mind as if it were happening once more. Notice how your new behaviour alters the whole experience and the reaction of any other people who may be in the memory, producing a more pleasing result.

9 If there is anything you do not like about the memory experiencing it in this new way go back to step 5 of this exercise and identify and create further resources which can be brought into the memory. (It can be helpful in this respect to imagine how someone you really admire would have coped with the situation in the memory, and then experience yourself feeling and acting that same way in your mind. As noted in Chapter 3, this role model exemplifying the desired behaviour can be someone you know, or a fictional character created in your imagination.)

10 When you feel satisfied with your memory (when you have made it the best it can be) let go of your anchor and open your eyes.

11 Think of that memory now and try to get back the 'old feeling'. Notice how much that number you chose to represent that bad feeling at the beginning of the exercise has gone down. (If you are not pleased with the end result you can go back to step 5 for more resources.)

Working with a memory generating feelings which are intense or traumatic

We will now look at ways you can work with a more traumatic memory which produces more intense negative feelings than those worked with in the preceding exercise. If your memory is usually represented in your mind by one main image the exercise to follow will be appropriate. However, the exercise after this one will be more suitable if the memory is stored in your mind like a mental film, made up of many consecutive images. I would strongly advise that if the memory you wish to work on produces very intense negative feelings, that you work on the following NLP techniques with the help of an experienced NLP therapist.

Exercise

1 Decide on a memory you wish to work with. When thinking of the memory notice what image comes into your mind.

2 If on a 'bad feelings' scale ranging from 1 to 10, 10/10 is as bad a feeling as you could feel, think of the number that represents how bad you feel as you look at this image.

3 Make yourself comfortable and close your eyes. Allow yourself to become aware of that memory in your mind.

4 Now we can experiment by making certain alterations to that image, similar to the method for working with stubborn negative thoughts (*see* Chapter 4). Take note of those alterations that make that bad feeling better or neutralize it completely.

5 You can experiment with the following manipulations, always returning the image back to 'normal' before testing a new alteration:

Colour Turn it to black and white, or brighten the colours.

Distance Push it further away or bring it closer.

Clarity Make it more blurred or more sharply focused.

Sound Put in extra sound (eg nice music) or take out the sound. Experiment with the volume.

Perspective Take yourself outside the image (dissociated) and look at yourself in the image from that perspective. Alternatively, be in the image (associated).

Humour For example, if there are other people in the memory, dress them up as clowns! Be creative!

This list is not comprehensive. You may think of other alterations you can make until your experimentation has given you a number of alterations that helped the negative feelings.

6 Now breathing slowly and deeply, view the memory bringing together all the manipulations that neutralize or improve that negative feeling. For instance, it may be that turning the image to black and white, pushing it away, softening the focus and being dissociated from the image

neutralizes the feeling. (If you still feel a degree of negativity in excess of what you can comfortably handle, go back to the experimentation stage once more.)

7 See the image this 'new' way in your mind five times in succession, opening your eyes after each viewing.

8 Now look at your 'old' way of remembering the memory (if your mind will allow you to!) and notice overall how much that number you chose to represent the bad feeling at the beginning has gone down. You should feel less negative than before, or ideally, neutral about that memory. If not go back to step 5. A change in the way you feel can transfer to a change in the way you behave from now on.

A case study illustration can give you an idea how this very useful technique can work in practise. I remember using this technique with a client who did not like leaving her home in case she would have the need to use a public bathroom. She said she would suffer from a sense of claustrophobia and panic attacks in public bathrooms.

We were able to uncover a memory (*see* Chapter 8) of when she was seven years old, in hospital to have her tonsils out. The old way of anaesthetizing patients, a mask over the mouth for the inhalation of ether, was a terrifying experience to that small child. She remembered the room she was in; it had cream-coloured tiles and pipes running along the wall, a bit like some bathrooms! Also this room had no windows. As an adult she found it impossible to enter any public bathroom without a window, no matter how urgent the call of nature!

It is quite possible that at some level of her mind this lady had linked the sense of terror and panic to her surroundings in the hospital, and that this then later generalized to public bathrooms. Thirty-eight years later this fear was still being triggered in her mind as she entered a bathroom in a public place.

We used the technique by getting her to visualize in her mind that memory of when she was in hospital. She experienced a score of 8/10 on a 'panic' scale (10/10 being the most panic she had ever felt). Quickly, I got her to experiment with certain alterations to the memory and we took note of those that helped to calm the feeling of panic.

When we put these positive manipulations of the memory together we finished up with my client seeing herself in a wider room with windows in her mind. There was white flowered wallpaper, and the hospital staff wore bright pink garments! In the background she chose to hear her favourite song (*Morning Has Broken*). She felt 0/10 on the 'panic' scale viewing the memory in this way.

The following week she told me how she had 'tested herself' by going into many public toilets around the city and in large department stores. She reported that the 'new way' of seeing her hospital memory came into her mind before entering each one. Once inside, if she did not like the way the bathroom looked (for example, if it had no windows), she just imagined it the way she would have liked it to be, and pretended it was this way! This allowed her to feel calm and carry on as normal. She described herself as 'a different me'.

Some people find that their memory cannot be represented effectively by one image, but that it is stored in their mind like a mental film, made up of many consecutive images. The following NLP technique is appropriate for such a memory and is particularly noted for its effectiveness with phobias and traumatic memories.

Exercise

1 Decide on a memory you wish to work with.
2 Think of a number out of ten on a 'bad feelings' scale to represent how bad you feel about this memory (10/10 being as bad as it could feel).
3 Make yourself comfortable, close your eyes and imagine you are sitting in a cinema looking at a blank screen.
4 Now begin seeing the memory on the screen, starting at the point before the negative feelings begin. Hold that very first image on the screen and have it there in black

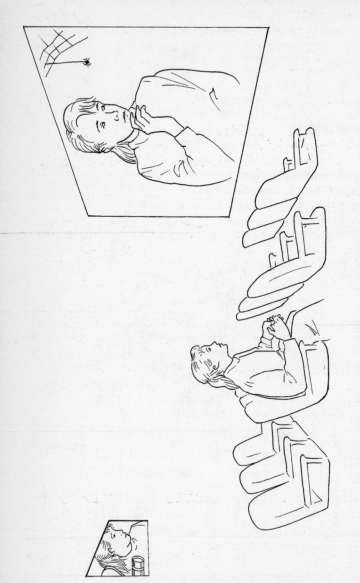

Figure 8 From the perspective of the projection room looking at yourself in the cinema viewing yourself on the screen

and white. Imagine that you are floating out of your body and up into the projection room of the cinema, so that you are looking at yourself in the cinema looking at yourself on the screen (*see* figure 8)

5 From the projection room push a button on the projector that allows the mental film to run. Watch it all from start to finish in black and white from the perspective of the projection room. Hold the last picture of the memory on the screen.

6 Now jump from the projection room and float into that last picture of the memory on the screen. Turn the picture to colour and rewind the whole film backwards at top speed within one second.

7 Repeat steps 5 and 6 five times.

8 Now float into your body sitting on the cinema seat and watch the film from start to finish in black and white. Breathe slowly and deeply, noting how much that initial number out of ten has gone down. Experiment if necessary with any other alterations (*see* previous technique) to lessen further or neutralize the negative feeling.

This technique is said to work by destroying the habitual pattern of the memory. By rewinding the film very quickly, there appears to be a confusion or deletion of the trigger function of the initial image of the sequence. Repeat the technique in the future if the immediate positive effect wears off.

CONFRONTING ANXIETY AND FEAR IN THE PRESENT

Having worked on any memories of the past that you feel have been adversely affecting you, you will now be in a better position to face and deal with the situations or objects of your fear in the present.

The need to take risks

The most important aspect of the treatment of fear is exposure to that fear. The more you avoid the situation or object of your fear the more your anxiety develops. This in turn encourages further avoidance behaviour. Your world becomes more and more limited as you take fewer and fewer risks. Things snowball as you attempt to protect your self-esteem from what you perceive as the probability of failure – the chance that you will be unable to handle your anxious feelings if they arise.

Albert Ellis (1962) in his *Guide to Rational Living* points out that one unrealistic expectation which causes much distress in this world is that we should do everything perfectly. Rather than insisting on feelings of comfort and demanding a 'perfect performance' every time you take a risk, it can be more helpful to look on the occasion as an opportunity to practise the coping skills outlined in this book. Confronting discomfort can provide you with practise for directly dealing with your fears.

Therefore each time you have the courage to take a risk, regardless of the outcome, you can feel good about yourself. Just taking the risk is beneficial. It is a 'win/win' situation. As noted by Pam, a recovering agoraphobic: 'I still feel apprehensive about going to certain places, but I'll usually have a go. I feel very pleased with myself when I've done something or gone somewhere that frightens me.' The only failure possible is an unwillingness to take that risk in the first place.

Knowing you can cope with the worst

When confronting anxiety and fear it may be helpful to ask yourself the following questions:

- What could be the worst possible outcomes of this?
- How likely are these outcomes?
- Could I live with these outcomes?

This is employing what Dr David Burns (1990) terms the 'What-if-Technique', whereby you push your fears to their worst extreme in your imagination. If you decide you could live with these outcomes then you have set yourself free.

Let's say you have a fear of embarrassing yourself in public. If your worst fear is realized, you might think, 'They'll all think I'm stupid'. But consider these points:

- Are they really likely to be thinking and talking of you in this way?
- If they are, does it really matter?

The truth is that in general people will not waste their time judging you and gossiping about you, and there is no point in wasting your time thinking about those who might! What is most important is how you feel about yourself. You are never going to win out if you want the approval of everyone around you. I don't know anyone who is loved by everybody!

Facing anxiety and fears in this way will frequently show them up to be not nearly as bad as you imagined. It helps to put things into perspective.

Systematic desensitization

Depending on the level of your anxiety or fear it may be advisable to work through the following technique with a trained therapist. Rather than being suddenly exposed to the situation or object that induces the problem (a process known as 'flooding'), a standard technique known as 'systematic desensitization' can be of use. This invaluable method involves a more gradual step-by-step approach. Although not essential it can be particularly beneficial to practise the following exercise while in the hypnotic state (*see* Chapter 6). Work through it over the coming weeks and months.

Exercise

1 Construct a target ladder of ten rungs ranging from the least-anxiety-producing step to the most-anxiety-producing step. For example, if you are suffering from agoraphobia it may be that you construct a ladder similar to the following:

i) Putting on a coat in preparation for going outside.

ii) Standing at the front door.

iii) Taking a few steps away from the front door while in the company of a friend.

iv) Taking a few steps away from the front door on your own.

v) Walking down to a small local shop and back with a friend.

vi) Walking down to a small local shop and back alone.

vii) Travelling a longer distance to larger shops in the company of a friend.

viii) Travelling a longer distance to larger shops alone.

ix) Staying in a crowded shopping centre for 5 minutes with a friend.

x) Staying in a crowded shopping centre for 5 minutes alone.

Construct your own ladder with steps that are tailored to your own situation.

2 When comfortably relaxed, practise in your imagination the first step of the ladder. See it and experience it in your mind in as much detail as possible. Use positive suggestions and imagery to help keep yourself calm. If you become uncomfortable at any point, abandon the scene in your mind temporarily and focus on allowing your breath to become calmer and relaxed once more before returning to the step.

3 Only when you feel comfortable in your imagination with that step, carry it out in reality. (It is preferable to do this immediately after your relaxation session.)

4 Practise your first step several times in reality until you feel confident to move on to the second step and then work in the same way.

5 Progress up the ladder at your own pace, always ensuring you are comfortable with the step in your imagination

before carrying it out in reality. There is a temptation to want to move too quickly ahead – resist it!

6 After you have completed each step, reward yourself in some way.

CHAPTER 8

Exploring Deeper

Don't feel discouraged if you don't immediately feel totally
successful ... many of us have some underlying feelings and
attitudes which can slow us down in our efforts...

Shakti Gawain

As noted in Chapter 3, when suffering with an anxiety disorder it is important to have realistic expectations regarding the rate at which improvement will occur. However,
what if you have been working on yourself for some time,
but still seem no nearer to achieving your goals? If this is
the case it may well be, as already discussed, that there are
some benefits to your situation and/or underlying reasons
for your behaviour that you are consciously unaware of
which need to be addressed. At this point help from a
trained therapist can be particularly useful. As this chapter
will show, there is also a lot you can do for yourself.

UNCOVERING IMPORTANT INFORMATION

One method often used to help uncover information from
the deeper part of the mind has been outlined by Bresler
(1990). In our everyday lives most of us are familiar with
experiencing a form of communication from a deeper,
usually wiser, part of ourselves. We often refer to this as a

'gut feeling' or 'intuition'. Bresler's approach, known as 'the inner adviser technique', involves giving voice and form to this inner wisdom in the imagination when the subject is in a comfortable, relaxed state. Allow yourself to work at an easy pace through the following exercise.

Exercise

1 Close your eyes and allow yourself to become comfortably relaxed. Visit your 'special place' for relaxation if you feel like it.

2 Allow yourself to visualize your inner adviser in your imagination. (For example, when I do this exercise I see my adviser as a wise old man similar to a picture of 'Merlin the Magician' I saw in a children's book many years ago! He has a long grey beard and wears flowing blue robes!)

3 Introduce yourself to your adviser. Apologize to him/her for not listening more in the past, and make it clear you will be more open to such communication in future.

4 Ask your adviser if he/she is willing to help you with the problem in hand. To avoid confusion in your mind as to what is truly the adviser's answer you may find it useful to ask the questions on your breath out (exhalation). The first response on your breath in (inhalation) can then be taken as your adviser's reply. Always thank your adviser for his/her answer.

5 If the reply to the question posed in the last step is positive, you can then ask whatever questions you feel are appropriate to help enhance insight into possible underlying reasons and 'secondary gains' or benefits associated with your anxious behaviour. There follows a sample of questions you may like to put to your adviser. After each question pause and allow an appropriate amount of time for your adviser's response.

- What is the cause of my anxiety disorder?
- What has stopped me from recovering? Are there any underlying problems I should be confronting and sorting out? What are they?
- What (if any) benefits am I getting from my present situation?

- How could I get these benefits in other more appropriate ways?
- What would you suggest I do to ensure recovery?
- Is there any other important information you would like me to be aware of? If so, what?

6 When you have finished thank your adviser for his/her help.

7 In your own time open your eyes allowing yourself to feel calm, inspired and alert!

There may be occasions when your adviser will not answer questions. One reason for this could be that he/she does not fully understand what you are asking. If this is the case it can be helpful to ask the same question in a number of different ways. If an answer is still not forthcoming it may be that your adviser is acting in a protective manner, not responding to your questions because he/she feels you are not ready to handle the replies at a conscious level. You may therefore ask your adviser what you need to do in order to be in a position to receive such information. If your adviser is adamant to keep the information at a subconscious level you will find the technique in the next section particularly useful since it allows work to be carried out with such information while keeping it out of conscious awareness.

NEGOTIATING WITH THE SUBCONSCIOUS MIND

There is a further method which can be of use when wishing to address the area of 'secondary gains' or benefits of an unwanted behaviour. Bandler and Grinder (1979) refer to the NLP technique to be outlined in this section as 'conscious reframing'. Consistent with the view expressed in this book the method makes the assumption that the part of the subconscious mind running your anxiety disorder sees the behaviour involved as serving a positive purpose or intention in some situation or context. Therefore that part of your subconscious mind will not pave a way forward for you to wave your disorder goodbye until a better alternative for achieving this positive purpose is found.

It may be compared to the problem of a mountain lying in the way of your desired destination. You may start climbing the steep rocky mountain path since you may see this as the only way of getting where you want to be. Then someone shows you a different and more appropriate way that you had overlooked – a path which travels around the mountain! You can obtain the same benefits (reach your destination) in a better way, and therefore you are in a position to abandon the original behaviour (climbing the steep mountain path).

The following exercise will guide you through the 'conscious reframing' technique in some detail. For a summary of the method *see* figure 9.

Exercise

1 Close your eyes and allow yourself to become comfortably relaxed. Visit your 'special place' for relaxation if you wish.

2 Express your appreciation to that part of your subconscious mind running your anxiety disorder for all it has been doing for you. (This may seem a strange thing to do but remember its intentions do have your best interests at heart!) Give that part of the subconscious mind a name; for instance, throughout this exercise I will refer to it as the 'anxiety disorder part'. You could say: 'I would like to thank you the "anxiety disorder part" of my subconscious mind for looking after me in the best way you know how.'

3 Establish communication signals from the 'anxiety disorder part' by asking: 'I would like you the "anxiety disorder part" to communicate with me in consciousness. Will you please show me a "yes" signal?' Allow yourself to be open and aware as you await the response. The signal can often present itself as a slight feeling which may be experienced anywhere in the body. A

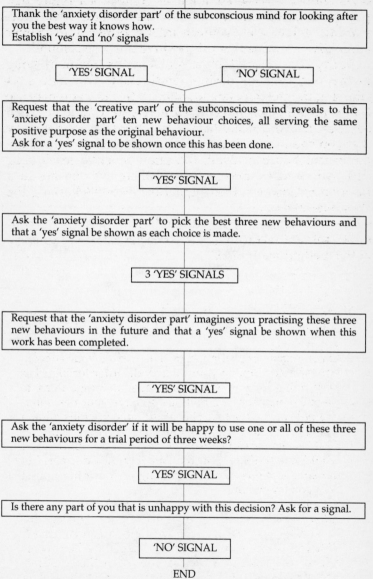

Figure 9 Summary of 'conscious reframing' exercise

valid response is one which cannot be controlled at will. (For example, one of my clients practising this technique experienced the signal as a definite tingling over her lip.) Once you feel you have received a response thank that 'anxiety disorder part'. Check to ensure you can not produce the same signal consciously. If you can, repeat the question until you are receiving a truly subconscious response.

4 Go through the last step again, this time to set up a definite and clear 'no' signal. You are now in a position whereby you can ask that part of your subconscious mind any question that can be responded to with a 'yes' or 'no'. (Always remember to thank that deeper part of your mind for all signals shown throughout the exercise.)

5 Suggest to the 'anxiety disorder part' that things can be better than they have been. You could say: 'I know the behaviour you run serves some very positive purpose for me, and I would like to suggest that things can be even better. Perhaps there is another behaviour which would serve the very same positive purpose that may be more appropriate.'

6 Whether or not we are aware of it we can all be creative at certain times in our lives. This step involves tapping into your creativity to help you with the problem at hand. Ask the 'anxiety disorder part' to communicate its positive purpose to the 'creative part' of the subconscious mind and to request that this part creates ten new behaviour choices which can all serve that same positive purpose. Request that the 'anxiety disorder part' shows you a 'yes' signal once it has been made aware at that level of these ten new behaviours. (Note: You will more than likely not be made consciously aware of these new behaviours.)

7 Ask that the 'anxiety disorder part' now choose three of these new behaviour choices ensuring that they are:
   i)   As good as or better than the original behaviour
   ii) Immediate and available
   iii) Appropriate to you in the life you wish to lead
   Request that a 'yes' signal be given each time a choice has been made.

8 Once you have received three 'yes' signals, thank the 'anxiety disorder part' and the 'creative part' for their work and co-operation.

9 Request that the 'anxiety disorder part' visualize you in the future practising these three new behaviours (and to notice how much better things can be as a result). Suggest it can use a 'yes' signal to show you when this work has been completed.

10 Ask the 'anxiety disorder part' if it will be happy to use one or all of these three new behaviours for a trial period of three weeks. Wait for the reply.

11 If the answer is 'yes', suggest that the result of this trial period can determine whether the new behaviour(s) are permanently taken on board. If the answer is 'no', assure the part that it can return to the old behaviour again if it is not satisfied with the results of the trial period. If the answer is still 'no', you can work through this whole exercise again with the part that objects.

12 Once you have received agreement on the trial period check that this situation is satisfactory to all other parts of you as follows: 'Is there any part of me that is not happy with the decision regarding the trial period with the new behaviour(s)?' Await a 'no' signal. (A 'yes' signal can be dealt with by going through the whole exercise with the part that objects.)

13 Open your eyes in your own time and allow yourself to feel calm, inspired and alert!

Because the identity of the new behaviour(s) taken on board for a trial period is generally kept at a subconscious level, consciously you can feel secure in the knowledge that whatever the behaviour, it will be at least as good as or better than the original. As noted prior to the exercise, since the new behaviour(s) can serve the same positive purpose or benefits as the unwanted behaviour, you are now in a better position to let go of that old behaviour (provided the trial period is seen through with a positive result).

If the original behaviour comes back after the three

weeks it can signify that the new behaviour choices were not sufficient to satisfy the purpose or intention of the 'anxiety disorder part'. It will at that point be necessary to go back to the 'creative part' and ask for three more choices of behaviour.

CHAPTER 9

Further Ways to Help You Capture a Sense of Freedom

The cure of the part should not be attempted without treatment of the whole.

Plato

In this chapter we will consider some of the many further practical ways you can help to improve your situation as an anxiety sufferer. So far our main focus has been on a psychological approach to anxiety. This has included outlining ways you can use your mind to actively calm the body. The latter half of this chapter will involve addressing the other side of the coin: the many positive ways you can work with the body to the benefit of your state of mind.

SLOWING DOWN

When feeling anxious it is easy to fall into the trap of speeding up in an attempt to put an end to the uncomfortable feelings as quickly as possible. However, the more you hurry the more likely it is that the anxiety will snowball. You will find it more helpful to slow everything down. Do your best to move slowly and calmly and reduce the pace of your thinking.

It also makes sense to make fewer demands on yourself.

Prioritize your activities and allow yourself short breaks throughout the day. Give yourself the time necessary to become absorbed and involved in activities you enjoy and find therapeutic, such as working in the garden or baking a cake!

BEING ASSERTIVE

Dr Burns (1990) notes how he believes anxiety and panic result from repressed negative feelings. In the same vein as psychoanalytic theory (*see* Chapter 2) he states that you can start to feel anxious and panicky when you avoid the conflicts that are worrying you. When you confront these problems the anxiety will frequently diminish or disappear. This can include becoming more assertive.

Assertive people communicate what they think and feel. They can say 'no'. Allowing their needs and problems to be known they confront conflicts, not in an aggressive way, but in a firm, polite manner. The rights of others as well as their own are respected. They take responsibility for their own wants rather than hoping that others will mind-read.

Assertiveness, like any skill, can be learnt and practised. If you feel you need help with your communication skills, why not enrol on an assertiveness training course?

FORGIVING YOURSELF AND OTHERS

Forgiveness is one of the most important virtues you need to acquire in order to become a calmer person. When you withhold forgiveness *you* suffer; a lot of the time the 'offender' does not even know the torment you are putting yourself through! They continue to enjoy life while you clutter your soul with unpleasant feelings. Blaming others is a pointless exercise.

Sometimes forgiving yourself can be even harder than forgiving others. If you have not forgiven yourself for something in the past. I would like to suggest you have suffered enough. How will prolonging the agony help things? You have a choice: you can chain yourself to the trauma of the past, or you can get on with your life.

LIVING IN THE NOW

So many people postpone happiness: 'When such and such happens, *then* I'll be happy!' What about right now?! We do not know how long we have on this planet and I do not believe that this is a dress rehearsal, so why not make the most of every moment? Dr Stanton (1983) recommends considering each day as a life in itself, stretching from the time you wake until bedtime. You can shape it in any way you choose.

All you have is now – the past is over and done with, the future has yet to happen. Whatever you are doing, enjoy the present moment.

KEEPING A DIARY

Living in the now is so much easier if your mind is clear. Unclutter your brain and become more organized by using a diary to write down things you need to remember. You may also decide to use one to monitor how you are positively progressing over the weeks as you practise the contents of this book. For example, you could make a note of those situations or incidents that you feel you are handling in a calmer way than you would have done in the past. Recording the beneficial results can help to motivate and encourage you to continue working on your mind.

CHANGING YOUR COMPANY

For the most part, we are all very susceptible to the influence of the people around us. Friendships with positive people teach you how to be positive; from those with negative people you learn how to be negative. Decide what you want from your life, and then choose your friends accordingly.

HAVING A LAUGH

Norman Cousins (1979) tells how he helped himself recover from a crippling illness by using laughter as his main medicine. Laughter helps you to free yourself from negative emotions. Confronting anxiety and problems with humour can really enrich your life. Watch films and read books that make you laugh. Listen to jokes. Get seriously into humour!!

WATCHING WHAT YOU EAT

The food you eat can play an important role in either increasing or decreasing symptoms of anxiety. Foods to generally avoid can include:

- Sweet foods (foods containing simple sugar, such as biscuits, cakes and ice-cream)
- Caffeine (found in coffee, black tea, soft drinks and chocolate)
- Dairy products (such as cheese, yoghurt and milk)
- Alcohol

Eating a well-balanced diet including fresh fruit and vegetables, nuts, starches, fish, meat and poultry (in moderation) can help to strengthen your body's ability to withstand stress. Foods rich in Vitamin B Complex, Vitamin C, Vitamin E, magnesium, potassium, calcium, zinc and phosphorus (*see* figure 10) are claimed to be helpful in relieving stress. Herbs such as passion-flower, chamomile, lemon balm, bay and wild cherry are also noted for their calming effect. (Note: If already taking another drug consult your doctor.)

Vitamin/Mineral	*Good dietary source*
Vitamin B Complex	Yeast Meat Wholegrain cereals Vegetable proteins (eg soya beans)
Vitamin C	Most fruit Green vegetables Liver Kidney Potatoes
Vitamin E	Most vegetable oils Nuts Seeds Lettuce
Magnesium	Nuts Soya beans Wholegrain cereals Green, leafy vegetables
Potassium	Fresh fruit Vegetables Wholegrain cereals
Calcium	Green, leafy vegetables Dairy products Nuts Beans Lentils
Zinc	Nuts Potatoes Rye Oats Garlic
Phosphorous	Nuts Wholegrain cereals Fish, meat and poultry Legumes

Figure 10 Good dietary sources for Vitamins/Minerals claimed to be helpful in relieving stress

It is helpful to become aware of how the food you consume may affect your mood. What you eat can make a difference to how you feel. Gradually substitute 'anxiety triggering foods' with healthier choices.

TAKING EXERCISE

The 'fight-or-flight' reaction mobilizes reserves of energy in the body in preparation for action. However, because many people 'stay with stress' this can result in excess energy being stored in the muscles in the form of increased tone. Exercising can provide a means of releasing this tension. It also serves the added beneficial function of releasing endorphins into the bloodstream (the body's own natural 'feel good hormones') which can explain the sense of well-being that can be experienced after exercise.

As stated earlier, it is a great deal easier to mentally relax if your body is relaxed. Additionally, concentrating on what you are doing while exercising can often result in distraction from life's stresses and worries. Dr Egil Martinsen (1990), on reviewing the appropriate literature, concludes: 'Available data indicate that regular physical exercise deserves a place in comprehensive treatment programmes for anxiety and depression.'

Before embarking on an exercise programme I would recommend you speak to your doctor. Panic attack suffers should be aware that some of the effects of exercising (for example, rapid breathing) may remind you of the effects of attacks. Build up your exercise programme gently.

TREATING YOURSELF TO A MASSAGE

Another method of releasing the build-up of tension from stress is through touch. A good massage can relax tight muscles, ease aches and pains and improve circulation. I would highly recommend you treating yourself to a professional massage whenever you can afford it. In between times a partner or friend may oblige.

You can also practise some 'self-massage' techniques. For example, to help ease a headache or a general feeling of strain you may wish to work in the following way: using gentle stroking movements, work from the centre of the forehead over in the direction of the temple and then upwards towards the hairline, one hand following the other.

USING ACUPRESSURE

Anxiety and its physical symptoms can also be transiently alleviated by acupressure: the application of pressure to specific acupuncture points on the body. In traditional Chinese medicine the belief is that energy (or Qi) circulates throughout the body through channels called meridians. In health, this energy flows smoothly, whilst during illness it becomes imbalanced. As with acupuncture, the aim of acupressure is to address this imbalance, restoring a harmonious flow of energy in the body.

For example, a stress-related headache, which extends from the back of the neck to the top of the head, can be relieved by pressure on two points at the base of the skull, using the thumbs. As can be seen in figure 11, these points lie at the junction of the neck and the skull on either side of the bony prominence (external occipital protuberance). Maintain pressure for five minutes or until headache is alleviated. Frontal headache can be alleviated by acupressure to each side of the temple, in the hollow just above and to the outside of the eyebrow (*see* figure 12).

Palpitations can be slowed by massaging the carotid sinus. This can be felt on the neck just behind the angle of the jaw, where the pulse is. Massage both sides as shown in figure 13 and this will slow the heart. Nausea can be alleviated by applying pressure to a point located approxi-

Figure 11 Points for relieving stress-related headache which extends from the back of the neck to the top of the head

Figure 12 Points for relieving frontal headache

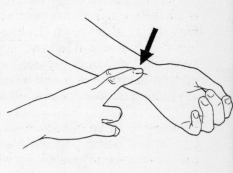

Figure 13 Point for relieving palpitations

Figure 14 Point for relieving nausea

mately two finger breadths from the crease of the wrist in the midline between the tendons on the side of the open palm (*see* figure 14). Massage the point on the right with the left hand and vice versa for a few minutes each. (There are wrist bands with studs on them available which, when placed over this point, serve to control motion sickness.)

BEING AWARE OF YOUR POSTURE AND FACIAL EXPRESSION

It was noted in Chapter 4 how negative thoughts can ruin your mood. It may also be true that your physiology has a direct effect on how you feel. It was William James, a famous psychologist at Harvard during the late 1800s, who first put forward the theory that the emotion we feel is the result of feedback from bodily changes.

Let us do an experiment. Drop your shoulders and look downwards with a serious expression on your face for about 20 seconds. Notice how you feel. I would guess your mood dampened slightly? Similarly, you'll probably notice an obvious improvement in your mood if you sit up tall, looking up and smiling. Test that for yourself now.

The acceptance of the effects of body changes on mood is even reflected in our everyday language, when we say for example that we are 'feeling down' or 'things are looking up'. So, next time you appear in a bad mood, if it seems to be for no apparent reason, check your posture and facial expression and alter them accordingly to help alter how you feel in a positive way.

Working with your body as well as your mind can help you to feel better physically and mentally. Taking better care of yourself in general can work towards helping you to feel more in charge of your life. It is good to know there is so much you can do to help to keep anxiety under control!

CHAPTER 10

Help from Professionals and Friends

Humans fear being humiliated and overwhelmed with feeling more than they fear death … Courage is daring to feel the incredible vulnerability of being human.

Tom Rusk and Randy Read

While you work on yourself you may feel it appropriate to reach out from time to time for some additional help, guidance and support. If your condition is particularly severe you may decide to do this sooner rather than later. In this chapter we will briefly explore the help available.

MEDICAL TREATMENT

As noted in Chapter 2, drug therapy should never be used as a substitute for counselling or psychotherapy in the management of anxiety and related disorders. However, that is not to disregard the fact that medication is appropriate in certain circumstances. For example, if anxiety symptoms are so severe that a person cannot function and carry out normal daily pursuits, short-term drug therapy can be useful.

Toxic side-effects, and even drug addiction, are possible consequences of the taking of high doses and long-term use of many drugs prescribed in the management of anxiety. Therefore, before agreeing to accept medication it can be helpful to discuss a number of areas, including the following, with your doctor:

- What are the risks/potential side-effects of the medication?
- What are the possible benefits?
- Are there any restraints to normal activities you should be aware of? (For instance, if the drug is likely to make you drowsy you should not drive.)
- For what length of time does your doctor plan to keep you on the medication? Will the chance of possible withdrawal effects be avoided?

If you are on medication, consult your doctor before you cut down or stop taking it. It is vital that you do this gradually so as to lessen the likelihood of possible withdrawal effects.

Up until the 1960s (if anxiety was treated at all) barbiturate drugs were recommended. These, however, fell into disrepute because of their adverse side-effects and their danger in overdose. Today three classes of drugs are considered for the management of anxiety: minor tranquillizers (anxiolytic agents), anti-depressants and beta blockers. We will now look briefly at each of these.

Minor tranquillizers (anxiolytic agents)

The benzodiazepine drugs – for example, Chlordiazepoxide (Librium), Diazepam (Valium) and Lorazepam (Ativan) – fall into this class. They are, at present, the most widely prescribed medication for anxiety. Benzodiazepines act by depressing the central nervous system, particularly that part of the brain under involuntary control (the limbic system).

The difference between specific benzodiazepines relates to their duration of action and the relative degree of sedation. Consequently some are used as sleeping pills, while others are used as anti-anxiety drugs. In both situations short-term use only is advised (two weeks or less). Long-term use can result in the individual becoming dependent on the drug and the medication may also start to lose its positive effect (sedation or anxiolysis). Side-effects can include fatigue, drowsiness, confusion and 'hangover' type effects. In some cases the very symptoms you wish to treat can occur initially as a reaction to the drugs. Therefore occasionally the anxiety may increase before any improvement is noticed.

Anti-depressant drugs

Many patients suffering with anxiety are put on anti-depressants, the rationale behind which is that there is a lot of overlap between anxiety disorders and depression. There are a large number of anti-depressants available, the most widely used being tricyclic anti-depressants, for example, Amitriptyline (Elavil), Imipramine (Tofranil), Doxepin (Sinequan), Nortriptyline (Aventyl) and Desipramine (Norpramin). A newer group which tends to have less in the way of side-effects than the tricyclic anti-depressants includes such drugs as Fluoxetine Hydrochloride (Prozac) and Paroxetine (Seroxat).

Anti-depressants are thought to act by increasing the level of certain neurotransmitters (chemicals which allow transmission from one nerve cell to another and consequently have profound effects on mood, appetite, sleep etc) in the brain. Tricyclic anti-depressants may take up to two weeks to have a beneficial effect. Side-effects are common, and can include drowsiness, dry mouth, blurred vision, difficulty passing urine, constipation, palpitations, an irregularity of heart rhythm and occasionally tremors in the hands. Generally, anxiety and depressive symptoms will improve together although in some cases anxiety may continue for some time after the depression has lifted.

Unlike the benzodiazepines, these drugs are not physically addictive.

Beta blockers

Beta blockers are commonly used in the management of anxiety. They act by helping to reduce hyperactivity of the sympathetic nervous system (the part of the nervous system responsible for the 'fight-or-flight' response) and therefore tend to inhibit some of the physical manifestations of anxiety (for instance, flushing, tremor and palpitations). This can help to break the self-perpetuating spiral of anxiety described in Chapter 1 (where misinterpretation of physical manifestations increase levels of anxiety which in turn increase physical manifestations).

One of the most commonly prescribed beta blockers is Propranolol (Inderal). Side-effects can include light-headedness, fatigue, drowsiness, nausea and lowering of blood pressure. Prescription on a regular basis may result in the occurrence of withdrawal effects if the medication is not stopped gradually.

A relatively new drug which does not fall into any of the preceding categories is called Buspirone Hydrochloride (BuSpar). It is becoming the most popular choice for many people suffering from a generalized anxiety disorder. It is thought to act at specific receptor sites in the brain. This drug is not physically addictive and does not cause excessive drowsiness. Side-effects can, however, include dizziness, insomnia and nervousness.

PSYCHOTHERAPY

Irrational anxiety often needs treatment by someone experienced in psychotherapy. You may wish for your doctor to refer you to a therapist or you may wish to seek one out yourself. It will be important to ensure you find someone who is both genuine and professional. Because therapists vary in their length and quality of training, points to check out with a prospective therapist include:

- How long was their training and what qualifications do they hold?
- Are they registered, and if so with which organization?
- How long have they been practising?
- What is their policy on payment for sessions? (I would be a bit uneasy about a therapist who charges for a set number of sessions in advance. It will not usually be possible for a therapist to gauge accurately how many sessions will be required at the outset.)
- Do they have experience of working with anxiety disorders?

The early work will include taking your full history, assessing your symptoms and deciding, with you, on the best approach for your treatment. The therapist will work with you on confronting and dealing with any possible underlying issues causing or maintaining your symptoms, and will teach you how to change unhelpful thoughts and beliefs. Periods of treatment will vary from person to person as they are tailored to the specific needs of the individual.

The organizations listed at the back of this book under the heading 'Hypnotherapy and NLP' will provide you with further information, and many can let you have a list of qualified practitioners in your area. In addition to ensuring you feel confident about the therapist's professional background, it will also be important to the success of your treatment that you like and feel comfortable with this person.

FAMILY AND FRIENDS

An important aspect of dealing with anxiety is to be able to talk about it and ask for help if necessary from those around you. Often less complicated problems can be put in a more positive light after a calm chat with someone willing to listen. Sometimes, however, strange as it may sound, and particularly in the case of phobics, too much kindness, help and support from those around you can add to the problem rather than alleviate it.

If the amount of this help can be 'restricted' appropriately, it can allow more space for you, as a phobic, to gain confidence and nurture a sense of independence as you confront feelings of discomfort. Too little care and too much protection are both counter-productive. Also, questions from those around you such as 'Are you okay?' or 'Are you going to be able to cope?' should be avoided as they draw attention to any symptoms present.

It may be productive for family and friends to read this book so that they are aware of the ways you will be working on yourself and can help you in your efforts. They can keep you encouraged, reassured and motivated throughout your journey.

SELF-HELP ORGANIZATIONS

Many people like to join lay groups of people who have problems similar to their own. As well as using the information service often provided by such organizations, sufferers can befriend other members who can share with them common experiences and coping tips. If the organization is dedicated to overcoming problems and moving onto solutions rather than just 'complaint swopping' you may well benefit from such support. (You will find a list of some self-help organizations presently operating at the back of this book.)

CONCLUDING THOUGHTS

Coping with an anxiety disorder can be a lonely and isolating experience. The fact is you are not on your own; you are one of many sufferers. My wish is that this book can act as a support and guide as you work towards recovery. Select the concepts that work best for you and gradually develop your own treatment plan.

As outlined in Chapter 3, to become that calmer person you wish to be you need to *want* to change and be committed to putting in the required effort. There is no magic wand; it is up to you. So, are you going to leave your life as it is or are you going to take positive action? I wish you well with it all.

> *You are never given a wish*
> *without also being given*
> *the power to make it true.*
> *You may have to work for it however.*
>
> Richard Bach

FURTHER READING

RECOMMENDED BOOKS

Bandler, R, *Using Your Brain for a Change*, Real People Press, 1985
Burns, D D, *The Feeling Good Handbook*, A Plume Book, 1990
Coleman, V, *Stress and Relaxation*, Hamlyn, 1993
Jeffers, S, *Feel the Fear and Do It Anyway*, Arrow Books, 1991
Peiffer, V, *Positive Thinking*, Element Books, 1994
Sheehan, E, *Health Essentials: Self-Hypnosis. Effective Techniques for Everyday Problems*, Element Books, 1995
Stanton, H E, *A Guide to More Relaxed Living. The Stress Factor*, MacDonald Optima, 1983

REFERENCES

Bach, R, *Illusions. The Adventures of a Reluctant Messiah*, Pan Books, 1977
Bandler, R, and Grinder J, *Frogs into Princes. Neuro-Linguistic Programming*, Eden Grove, 1979
Bowlby, J, *Separation, Attachment and Loss, Vol 2*, New York: Basic Books, 1973
Bresler, D E, *Meeting an Inner Adviser*, in: D C Hammond (Ed), *Handbook of Hypnotic Suggestions and Metaphors*, An American Society of Clinical Hypnosis Book, W W Norton & Co, 1990
Caddy, E, *The Dawn of Change*, Findhorn Press, 1979
Clark, D M, Salkovskis, P M, Hackmann, A, Middleton, H, Anastasiades, P, and Gelder, M, *A Comparison of Cognitive Therapy, Applied Relaxation and Imipramine in the Treatment of*

Panic Disorder, British Journal of Psychiatry, 164:759–769, 1994

Collier, J (ed), *Psychological Treatment for Anxiety – An Alternative to Drugs? Drug and Therapeutics Bulletin*, The Independent Review For Doctors And Pharmacists From Consumers' Association, 31:73–74, 1993

Coryell, W, and Winokur, G, *The Clinical Management of Anxiety Disorders*, Oxford University Press, 1991

Cousins, N, *The Anatomy of an Illness*, W W Norton, New York, 1979

Ellis, A A and Harper, R A, *A Guide to Rational Living*, Institute for Rational Living, California, 1962

Eriksson, B O, Mellstrand, T, Peterson, L, Remstrom, P and Svedmyr, N, *Sports Medicine, Health and Medication*, Guinness Publishing, 1990

Gawain, S, *Creative Visualisation*, Bantam Books, 1982

Hambly, K, *Banish Anxiety*, Thorsons, 1991

Hay, L L, *The Power is Within You*, Eden Grove, 1991

Holmes, T H, and Rahe, R H, *The Social Re-adjustment Rating Scale*, Journal of Psychosomatic Research, 11:213–218, 1967

Jacobson, E, *Progressive Relaxation*, Chicago: University of Chicago Press, 1938, 1974

James, W, *The Principles of Psychology*, New York: Holt, 1890

Jencks, B, *Methods of Relaxed Breathing*, in: D C Hammond (Ed), *Handbook of Hypnotic Suggestions and Metaphors*, An American Society of Clinical Hypnosis Book, W W Norton & Co, 1990

Kabat-Zinn, J, Massion, A O, Kristeller, J, Peterson, L G, Fletcher, K E, Pbert, L, Lenderking, W R, and Santorelli, S F, *Effectiveness of a Meditation – Based Stress Reduction Program in the Treatment of Anxiety Disorders*, American Journal of Psychiatry, 149:936–943, 1992

Lazarus, R S, and Folkman, S, *Stress, Appraisal and Coping*, New York:Springer, 1984

Martinsen, E W, *Physical Fitness, Anxiety and Depression*, British Journal of Hospital Medicine, 43:194–199, 1990

Pavlov, I P, *Conditioned Reflexes*, New York: Oxford University Press, 1927

Prather, D C, *Promoted Mental Practice as a Flight Simulator*, Journal of Applied Psychology, 57:353–355, 1973

Roger, J, and McWilliams, P, *You Can't Afford The Luxury Of A Negative Thought*, Thorsons, 1991

Rusk, T, and Read, R *I Want to Change But I Don't Know How. A Step-by-step Programme for Mastering Life*, Thorsons, 1990

Snaith, P, *Clinical Neurosis. Second Edition*, Oxford University Press, 1991

Stafford-Clark, D, Bridges, P, and Black, D, *Psychiatry for Students. Seventh Edition*, Unwin Hyman, 1990

Watson, J B and Rayner, R, *Conditioned Emotional Reactions*, Journal of Experimental Psychology, 3:1–16, 1920

Yerkes, R M & Dodson, J D, *The Relation of Strength of Stimulus to Rapidity of Habit-formation*, Journal of Comparative and Neurological Psychology, 18:459–482, 1908

USEFUL ADDRESSES

The following addresses are provided for information purposes only, and are not necessarily a source of recommendation.

Hypnotherapy and neuro-linguistic programming (NLP)

Australia
Australian Society of Hypnosis
Austin Hospital
Heidelberg
Vic 3084

Australian Institute of NLP
PO Box 1
University of Queensland
St Lucia
Queensland 4067

Austria
Osterreichische Gesellschaft fur
Autogenes Training und Allge-
meine Psychotherapie
Testarellogasse 31/13
A-1130 Vienna

OTZ NLP
Teyberg 1/19
A-1140 Vienna

Belgium
Viaamse Vereniging voor
Autogene Training en
Hypnotherapy vzw
Gebroeders Verhaegenstr 13
2800 Mechelen

Institut Resources PNL
37 Bois Pirart
B-1320 Genval

Canada
Ontario Society of Clinical
Hypnosis
200 St Clair Ave W
Suite 402
Toronto ON M4V 1R1

NLP Centres of Canada
338 First Avenue
Ottawa
Ontario K1S 2G9

Germany
Deutsche Gesellschaft für
ärtzliche Hypnose und
Autogenes Training ev
Oberforstbacher Str 416
D-52076 Aachen

NLP Ausbildungs-Institut
Rathausplatz 7
D-69221 Dossenheim

Ireland
Irish Society of Clinical and
Experimental Hypnosis
c/o 59 McCurtain St
Cork

Israel
Israel Society for Clinical and
Experimental Hypnosis
44 Hanassl Avenue
Haifa 34643

The Israel Institute for NLP
16 Revivim Street
Tel-Aviv 69354

Italy
Associazione Medica Italiana per
10 Studio dell Ipnosi
Via Paisiello 28
20131 Milano MI

Italian Association of NLP
Via Bandello 18
20123 Milano

Norway
Norwegian Society of Clinical
and Experimental Hypnosis
The Pain Clinic
Bergen University Hospital
N-5021 Bergen

Interaction
PO Box 1266 Vika
N-0111 Oslo 1

South Africa
South African Society of
Clinical Hypnosis
29 Isabel Street
Kilner Park
XI, 0186

United Kingdom
The National Council Of
Psychotherapists
'The Hypnotherapy Register'
46, Oxhey Rd
Watford WD1 4QQ

British Hypnosis Research
1 King Street
Bakewell
Derbyshire
DE45 1DZ

British Society of Experimental
and Clinical Hypnosis
The Department of Psychology
Grimsby General Hospital
Scartho Road
Grimsby DN33 2BA

Association for Neuro-Linguistic
Programming
48 Corser St
Stourbridge DY8 2DQ

USA
The American Society of Clinical
Hypnosis
2200 East Devon Ave
Suite 291 Des Plaines
Illinois 60018

The National Association of
Neuro-Linguistic Programming
7126 Eastshea Boulevard
3B Scottsdale
Arizona 85254

Self-help organizations

Australia
Agoraphobia Support Group
P O Box 2090
North Brighton 3186
Tel: 5096193/7968744

Box Hill Group
Box Hill Community Health
Centre
65 Carrington Road
Box Hill 3128
Tel: 8902220

GROW
29 Erasmas Street
Surrey Hills 3127
Tel: 8909846

United Kingdom
The Open Door Association
c/o 447 Pensby Road
Heswall
Wirral
L61 9PQ
Tel: 0151 6482022

Panic attacks, phobias and
anxiety disorders (Pax)
4 Manor Brook
Blackheath
London SE3 9AW
Tel: 0181 3185026

The Phobics Society
4 Cheltenham Road
Chorlton-cum-Hardy
Manchester M21 9QN
Tel: 0161 8811937

Phobic Action
Hornbeam House
Claybury Grounds
Manor Road
Woodford Green
Essex IG8 8PR
Tel: 0181 5592551

Action on Phobias
6 Grange St
Kilmarnock
Ayrshire
Scotland KA1 2AR
Tel: 01357 22274

The Northern Ireland
Agoraphobia and Anxiety
Society
2131 Lisburn Rd
Belfast
Tel: 01232 235170

USA
Anxiety Disorder Association
6000 Executive Boulevard
Suite 513
Rockville
M D 20852
Tel: 1800 6472642

National Anxiety Foundation
3135 Custer Drive
Lexington
Kentucky 40517
Tel: 1800 7551576

Anxiety Disorders Resource
Center
Third Floor
79 Madison Ave
New York
N Y 10016
Tel: 212 2130909

If contacting any of the self-help organizations by post it would be advisable to enclose a stamped addressed envelope or an international reply coupon for their reply.

Index

acupressure 89–91
acupuncture 89
anti-depressant drugs 95–6
anxiety disorders, definition 3
anxiety disorders, causes
  anxiety as a learnt response
    10–11
  coping behaviour 13
  genetic disposition 9–10
  inner conflicts 10
  physical factors 12
  self-talk 12–13
  social determinants 13–15
  upbringing 10
assertiveness 84
autonomic nervous system 2, 27

beta blockers 96

'calm anchor' 46–8, 65–6
'classical conditioning' 11
cognitive therapy 16
'conscious reframing' 77–81
coping skills 70–1
cue cards 36

diet 86–7
drugs 17, 93–6

exercise 88

family help 97–8
'fight or flight' response 2, 3, 5,
  29, 88

generalized anxiety disorder
  (GAD) 4

herbs 86
hypnosis 52–5
hypnotherapy 52, 57, 97

keeping a diary 85

laughter as medicine 86
life event scale 14

massage 88–9
medical treatment 93–4
mental rehearsal 41–2

negative thoughts and actions
  overcoming them 29–31
  negative memories 61, 62, 63–4,
    65–68
  reframing 29–30
  stop method 32, 33
neuro-linguistic programming
  (NLP) 32, 34, 43, 63, 65, 67, 77,
  97

panic attacks 5, 20, 88
Pavlov, Ivan 11
phobias
  agoraphobia 6–7, 20, 23
  simple 7–8
  social 7
positive forward projection 42
positive friendship 85

positive thinking 28
positive visualization 34, 39–41
posture 91
progressive body relaxation 51–2
psychoanalytical theory 10, 84
psychological treatment 15, 16, 17
psychotherapy 17, 96–7

realism and recovery 21, 75
'reframing' 29–30
relaxation 16, 49–50
relaxed breathing 50–1

self-help organizations 105–108
self-hypnosis 16, 54, 55–60

self-hypnosis, precautions
    57–8
sexual anxiety 46
subconscious mind 27–8, 77–8
'swish' technique 43

therapy
    systematic desensitization 71,
    72, 73
    inner adviser technique 76, 77
tranquillizers 94, 95

vitamins 86, 87

what-if technique 71

ELEMENT BOOKS LTD
PUBLISHERS

Element is an independent general publishing house. Our list includes titles on Religion, Personal Development, Health, Native Traditions, Modern Thought and Current Affairs, and is probably the most comprehensive collection of books in its sphere.

To order direct from Element Books, or to join the Element Club without obligation and receive regular details of great offers, please contact:
Customer Services, Element Books Ltd, Longmead, Shaftesbury, Dorset SP7 8PL, England.   Tel: 01747 851339   Fax: 01747 851394

Or you can order direct from your nearest distributor:

UK and Ireland
Penguin Group Distribution Ltd,
Bath Road, Harmondsworth,
Middlesex UB7 0DA, England.
Tel: 0181 899 4000
Fax: 0181 899 4020/4030

Canada
Penguin Books Canada Ltd,
10 Alcorn Avenue, Suite 300,
Toronto, Ontario MV4 3B2.
Tel: (416) 925 2249
Fax: (416) 925 0068

Central & South America & the Caribbean
Humphrey Roberts Associates,
24 High Street,
London E11 2AQ, England.
Tel: 0181 530 5028
Fax: 0181 530 7870

USA
Viking Penguin Inc,
375 Hudson Street, New York,
NY 10014.
Tel: (212) 366 2000
Fax: (212) 366 2940

Australia
Jacaranda Wiley Ltd, PO Box
1226, Milton, Queensland 4064.
Tel: (7) 369 9755 Fax: (7) 369 9155

New Zealand
Forrester Books NZ Ltd,
3/3 Marken Place, Glenfield,
Auckland 10.
Tel: 444 1948   Fax: 444 8199

Other areas:
Penguin Paperback Export Sales,
27 Wrights Lane,
London W8 5TZ, England.
Tel: 0171 416 3000
Fax: 0171 416 3060

The Health Essentials Series

Comprehensive, high-quality introductions to complementary healthcare

Each book in the *Health Essentials* series is written by a practising expert in their field, and presents all the essential information on each therapy, explaining what it is and how it works. Advice is also given, where possible, on how to begin using the therapy at home, together with comprehensive lists of courses and classes available worldwide.

In this series:

Acupuncture, Peter Mole	ISBN 1 85230 319 0
The Alexander Technique, Richard Brennan	ISBN 1 85230 217 8
Aromatherapy, Christine Wildwood	ISBN 1 85230 216 X
Ayurveda, Scott Gerson	ISBN 1 85230 335 2
Chi Kung, James MacRitchie	ISBN 1 85230 371 9
Chinese Medicine, Tom Williams	ISBN 1 85230 589 4
Colour Therapy, Pauline Wills	ISBN 1 85230 364 6
Flower Remedies, Christine Wildwood	ISBN 1 85230 336 0
Herbal Medicine, Vicki Pitman	ISBN 1 85230 591 6
Kinesiology, Ann Holdway	ISBN 1 85230 433 2
Massage, Stewart Mitchell	ISBN 1 85230 386 7
Reflexology, Inge Dougans with Suzanne Ellis	ISBN 1 85230 218 6
Self-Hypnosis, Elaine Sheehan	ISBN 1 85230 639 4
Shiatsu, Elaine Liechti	ISBN 1 85230 318 2
Skin and Body Care, Sidra Shaukat	ISBN 1 85230 350 6
Spiritual Healing, Jack Angelo	ISBN 1 85230 219 4
Vitamin Guide, Hasnain Walji	ISBN 1 85230 375 1

128/144 pages • 216 x 138 mm • Paperback • Line illustrations
UK £5.99 • USA $9.95 • Canada $12.99

The Natural Way Series

Comprehensive guides to gentle, safe and effective treatments
for today's common illnesses

Element's innovative *Natural Way* series provides practical and authoritative information on holistic and orthodox treatments for our most common illnesses. Endorsed by both the British Holistic Medical Association and the American Holistic Medical Association, these concise guides explain clearly what the disease is, how and why it occurs, and what can be done about it. Each book includes advice on helping yourself and where to turn to for outside qualified help.

In this series:

Arthritis & Rheumatism, Pat Young .... ISBN 1 85230 629 7

Asthma, Roy Ridgway .... ISBN 1 85230 492 8

Back Pain, Helena Bridge .... ISBN 1 85230 581 9

Colds & Flu, Penny Davenport .... ISBN 1 85230 630 0

Diabetes, Catherine Steven .... ISBN 1 85230 705 6

Eczema, Sheena Meredith .... ISBN 1 85230 493 6

Heart Disease, Richard Thomas .... ISBN 1 85230 494 4

Irritable Bowel Syndrome, Nigel Howard .... ISBN 1 85230 583 5

Migraine, Eileen Herzberg .... ISBN 1 85230 495 2

Multiple Sclerosis, Richard Thomas .... ISBN 1 85230 715 3

Premenstrual Syndrome, Jane Sullivan .... ISBN 1 85230 805 2

128/144 pages • 178 x 111 mm • Paperback • Line illustrations
UK £3.99 • USA $5.95 • Canada $7.99